Hand that Rocks the Cradle

Hand that Rocks the Cradle

400 CLASSIC BOOKS FOR CHILDREN

by Nathaniel Bluedorn

March 2008
Christian Logic

Hand that Rocks the Cradle
by Nathaniel Bluedorn

Library of Congress Control Number: 2007909744
ISBN 978-0-9745315-4-0

Christian Logic
P.O. Box 46
Muscatine, Iowa 52761
309-537-3464
www.christianlogic.com

1993 First Edition
1996 Revised Second Edition
1998 Revised Third Edition
2002 Fourth Edition
2008 Fifth Edition

"...Thou shalt not steal,...Thou shalt love thy neighbour as thyself." – Romans 13:9 "Thou shalt not muzzle the ox that treadeth out the corn. And, The labourer is worthy of his reward." – 1 Timothy 5:18

FOR DAD AND MOM
BECAUSE YOU READ TO US

Reading Aloud

The year I turned five my mother read the *Little House* series to us kids. That began a long procession of books she and Dad read to us. The pictures I drew in my mind of those stories decorate my childhood memories. They molded me.

I want to help you to read to your children.

Why read to your children?

Stories broaden horizons. By listening, children experience more people and places than they might in their short childhood. On a cozy couch, parents can take the family *Around the World in Eighty Days* with Jules Verne.

Good books teach character. Charles Dickens describes villains in *Oliver Twist* that he contrasts with the innocent waif, Oliver – who is kidnapped by Fagin the thief-trainer. Authors teach good qualities by contrasting them with bad. Children learn values like curiosity, love, and adventure.

Listening comprehension comes before reading comprehension. Children learn to understand concepts and draw inferences from the stories they hear. Children who are read to have stronger language skills – larger vocabularies and improved memory and sequencing abilities. They learn to read difficult books sooner.

Reading teaches writing. Listening to E. B. White's *Charlotte's Web* imprints his style in a child's memory. Good books are the work of great minds. Listening to them teaches children what good writing sounds like.

Stories teach history. *The Scarlet Pimpernel* spurred me to learn about France and the Revolution. This led me to Napoleon and then the lost Louis XVII. Howard Pyle's *Men of Iron* teaches more about medieval life than any textbook. History is something to experience, and we do this in stories.

Reading aloud builds family bonds. It was comforting and reassuring to sit cozily next to my mother on a windy winter afternoon while she read to us Irving's *The Alhambra*. I remember our whole family listening suspended in our seats as Dad read Russell's *The Wreck of the Grosvenor*. Every time Dad asked if he should stop, we would shout for him to go on.

How to read aloud?

My mother read in the afternoon when school was done. She used reading aloud as a reward. She asked us to be somewhat quiet, but we could play with our toys or art.

She wanted us to ask questions when we did not understand something. Sometimes she asked questions to see if we were catching it all. Sometimes she asked us to retell what we heard at the end of a chapter; this is called narration.

Mother read for an hour or two depending on how soon her voice tired. Sometimes we would continue enwrapped by an exceptionally bonnie tale all afternoon long. In showing her love for reading, Mother catalyzed the love in us.

My dad read from a different book before bedtime. He read more action and adventure. There is something about Sherlock Holmes and stories like *Treasure Island* that lends them to being read in the evening.

Don't read boring books. Read books you're enthusiastic about yourself. Your kids will like them too. Challenge yourself to read books you think are difficult. It's like exercising your reading muscles. Young children may not seem to catch something at first, but the details have been tucked away in their memory.

Audio books are wonderful. Each performance adds a voice and interpretation to the reading. Our family has some favorite readers. Audio books can be good for road trips. If you feel intimidated by reading aloud, you might start with audio books.

What books to read?

What are the "classics"? If you ask a librarian, she will tell you the classics are books that have endured the test of time. (Some people get these confused with ancient Greek and Roman literature.) To me, classic books are ones that have found their way into the hearts and minds of readers for several generations. They've lasted.

Should you read only the classics? No. Not all classics are good for children. And there are good modern books that have not yet gathered enough dust to be called "classic."

I recommend avoiding light reading – books that use small vocabularies and don't develop their characters. Examples might be the *Hardy Boys* series, *Nancy Drew* series, or *The Boxcar Children*. I'd avoid abridged books also. If a book is good enough for your children, it is good enough to read in the author's original words.

For parents who have never read aloud, I recommend some simple stories that go off with a bang: *Penrod*, *The Door in the Wall*, *The Matchlock Gun*, *Johnny Tremain*, *King of the Wind*, or *The Wolves of Willoughby Chase*.

For parents who want to try something harder, I recommend *Hitty: Her First Hundred Years; Men of Iron; Lassie Come-Home; The Yearling; The Hobbit; Swallows and Amazons;* or *Swiss Family Robinson*.

For parents who really want a challenge, I recommend *The Moonstone*, *Les Misérables*, *Ivanhoe*, *The Black Arrow*, or *Ben-Hur*.

About This List

My mother kept this list of the books she and Dad read to us. My brother and sisters and I added books that we read ourselves. My family is conservative; many books didn't make it onto this list. We prefer older books, but we enjoy some newer books too. Almost every book listed here is fiction.

I have summarized the plot for each book. I hope I didn't give away too much.

BOOK SYMBOLS

⌛ Time the story takes place
🌐 Geographic setting of the story
© Publication date of the book

READING LEVELS

1 Language and plot are easy – all ages
2 Language is more difficult or plot more complex – ages 10 and up
3 Language is advanced or plot more mature – ages 13 and up

Reading levels help many parents. My mother didn't stick to these reading levels; I'll forgive you if you ignore them.

Finding books can be difficult. You can find some books at your local library. Most libraries have an interlibrary loan program that allows you to order books from other libraries. If you can't find a book at the library, look on the Internet.

I would like to thank my sister Johannah Stanford and my friend Bethany Notgrass for writing some of these reviews.

400 Classic Books for Children

Aesop

AESOP'S FABLES 1

⌛ ANCIENT TIME ⊕ GREECE © 620-560 BC

Some of Aesop's fables are familiar: "The Town Mouse and the Country Mouse," "The Boy Who Cried Wolf," and "The Tortoise and the Hare." Some may be new to readers: "The Fox and the Stork," "The Frog and the Mouse," and "The Lark and Her Young Ones." Each brief story concludes with a catchy moral, such as "The race is not always to the swift."

Aesop's fables make perfect family reading to spark discussion.

Aiken, Joan

THE WOLVES OF WILLOUGHBY CHASE 1

⌛ EARLY 1800S ⊕ ENGLAND © 1963

Little Sylvia goes to visit her rich cousin, Bonnie, who lives in a country manor. She arrives as her cousin's parents are leaving on a trip to the tropics. The governess left to care for them has designs on Bonnie's parents' estate. To rid herself of the girls, she says Bonnie's parents have died in a shipwreck and sends the girls to an orphanage. The girls run away to London and enlist the help of the family lawyer.

This book is one of my mother's favorites to read aloud. It is full of action, secret passageways, and villains.

Alcott, Louisa May

LITTLE WOMEN 2

⌛ 1860S ⊕ MASSACHUSETTS © 1869

The four March girls live with their mother while their father is away serving as a chaplain in the Civil War. This is the story of Meg, who works as a governess; tall, awkward Jo, who likes to write; saintly and contented Beth; and the youngest, dreamy Amy.

Largely autobiographical, this book is about Louisa's own sisters, with herself as Jo. This is one of the best-loved books of all time for children and grown-ups.

AN OLD-FASHIONED GIRL 2

⏳ MID-1800S 🌐 UNITED STATES © 1870

Polly has come to visit her friend Fanny, a wealthy city girl. Polly, who is from the country, dresses and behaves simply. This contrasts with Fanny and her fashionable friends. Fanny comes to love Polly for her willingness to be kind and true to herself – an old-fashioned girl.

LITTLE MEN 2

⏳ MID-1800S 🌐 MASSACHUSETTS © 1871

Jo and her husband Friedrich Bhaer run a school for boys. This is the story of their adventures. Mr. and Mrs. Bhaer manage their school family with love and good humor, helping their boys build good character. This is a sequel to *Little Women*.

JO'S BOYS 2

⏳ LATE 1800S 🌐 MASSACHUSETTS © 1886

The children introduced in *Little Women* and *Little Men* have grown up and are establishing their careers and getting married.

Aldrich, Thomas Bailey

THE STORY OF A BAD BOY 2

⏳ 1800S 🌐 NEW HAMPSHIRE © 1869

At the age of ten, Tom Aldrich is sent to live with his grandfather. His grandfather immediately sends him to the local grammar school to keep him out of trouble. Tom makes friends and also a few enemies. His escapades include appearing to shoot his friend with an arrow in the play *William Tell* and surprising the townsfolk from their beds by firing an old cannon. This is a story of how boys grew up in the 1800s.

Alger, Horatio

TOM THE BOOTBLACK 1

⌛ LATE 1800S 🌐 UNITED STATES AND ENGLAND
© 1869-1899

Horatio Alger wrote over a hundred stories about poor boys who by hard labor, good fortune, and virtue work their way out of misfortune and poverty. They are often reunited with a rich uncle or long-lost parent. These stories teach good character and the benefits of entrepreneurial business practices. Young boys used to eat up these books until they went out of style.

Andersen, Hans Christian

ANDERSEN'S FAIRY TALES 1

⌛ MIDDLE AGES-1800S 🌐 EUROPE © 1835-1873

Andersen retells European folk tales such as "The Tinder-Box," "The Princess and the Pea," and "Little Claus and Big Claus" that he heard as a boy. He also tells a few of his own stories, such as "Thumbelina," "The Little Mermaid," and "The Emperor's New Clothes."

Anonymous (James De Mille)

MARTYR OF THE CATACOMBS: A TALE OF ANCIENT ROME 2

⌛ ANCIENT TIME 🌐 ROME © 1858

Marcellus, a captain in the Praetorian Guard, becomes a Christian.

Austen, Jane

SENSE AND SENSIBILITY 3

⌛ EARLY 1800S 🌐 ENGLAND © 1811

Sisters Elinor and Marianne Dashwood are very different. Elinor is steady and prudent; Marianne is impulsive and demonstrative. Both sisters love men who treat them unfairly, and each reacts according to her character. Elinor and Marianne must learn the truth about themselves before they reach a happy ending. *Sense and Sensibility* stands out from other Austen novels because of its complex plot.

PRIDE AND PREJUDICE 3

⌛ EARLY 1800S 🌐 ENGLAND © 1813

There are five daughters in the Bennett family, and Mrs. Bennett has devoted herself to seeing them all well married. Elizabeth, the second eldest, tries to maintain some respectability through her mother's schemes and her sisters' romantic entanglements. She finds herself pursued by Mr. Darcy, the last man in the world she hoped to interest. This most famous of Jane Austen's novels sparkles with wit, wisdom, and brilliant use of the English language.

MANSFIELD PARK 3

⌛ EARLY 1800S 🌐 ENGLAND © 1814

Fanny Price is a poor relation invited into the Bertram household on charity. She lives on the sidelines of the family while developing a humble yet resolute character the others lack. Fanny watches as her adopted family members make dreadful mistakes and question her own decisions of conscience. This is the longest of Austen's novels and fully develops its characters and moral lessons.

EMMA 3

⌛ EARLY 1800S 🌐 ENGLAND © 1816

Emma has always been the center of attention. She thinks she is witty and wise. Everyone in her circle only confirms her pride, except for her friend Mr. Knightley, who cares for Emma too much to let her be foolish. Emma's floundering attempts to matchmake take her down a notch, until she is ready to listen to Mr. Knightley. An amusing book.

NORTHANGER ABBEY 3

⌛ EARLY 1800S 🌐 ENGLAND © 1818

Catherine Morland is an immature girl of seventeen who is invited to visit Bath with an elderly couple. There she meets the Tilney family, who love her and inspire her to improve herself. Jane Austen uses this playful book to poke fun at the absurdities in English society.

PERSUASION 3

⌛ EARLY 1800S 🌐 ENGLAND © 1818

Anne Elliot believes she is past hope of ever being loved. Years before, she was persuaded to end an attachment of true love. She has never met another man who compared with Captain Wentworth. He reenters her life by a coincidence, and she must face her old feelings for him. What are Captain Wentworth's feelings? The hero and heroine of this story are examples of character and moral courage.

Bagnold, Enid

NATIONAL VELVET 1

⌛ EARLY 1900S 🌐 ENGLAND © 1935

Velvet Brown wins her dream horse, a piebald colt, in a lottery and discovers that the horse is a good jumper. Mi, the hired hand, helps Velvet train the horse and enter the Grand National race – pretending to be a boy.

Bailey, Carolyn Sherwin

MISS HICKORY 1

⌛ 1800S 🌐 WOODS © 1947

Miss Hickory is a little woman made from an apple-wood twig and the head of a hickory nut. She survives several trying months alone in her corncob house. This is a humorous story inhabited by odd forest animals.

Baker, Olaf

SHASTA OF THE WOLVES 1

⌛ ANCIENT TIME 🌐 WESTERN AMERICA © 1919

Shasta is a lost Indian child who is raised by a wolf with her pups. He lives among the forest animals, until one day he discovers his native tribe.

I have always loved stories of America before the paleface made his appearance.

Barrie, J. M.

PETER PAN 1

⌛ 1800S 🌐 LONDON & NEVERLAND © 1911

Peter Pan visits London to listen to Mary Darling tell stories to her children at bedtime. The children spot Peter one night, and he loses his shadow while escaping. Wendy reattaches Peter's shadow, and Peter takes her to Neverland to be a mother to his gang of Lost Boys.

Beatty, Patricia

I WANT MY SUNDAY, STRANGER! 1

⌛ CIVIL WAR ⊕ UNITED STATES © 1977

A California Mormon boy travels the United States during the Civil War in search of his confiscated horse named Sunday.

This book is one of my mother's favorites to read aloud.

WAIT FOR ME, WATCH FOR ME, EULA BEE 1

⌛ 1860S ⊕ SOUTHWEST AMERICA © 1978

Lewallen is separated from his sister Eula Bee when they are taken captive in a Kiowa Indian raid. Lewallen escapes and tries to ransom his four-year-old sister from the Comanche.

This book is one of my mother's favorites to read aloud.

Bennett, John

MASTER SKYLARK 2

⌛ 1500S ⊕ ENGLAND © 1896

Because of his fine singing voice, Nick Attwood is kidnapped by a London stage-player. He is taught in a boy's school and eventually performs before the queen. In the end, Master Shakespeare helps Nick return home.

Though the author uses an excessive number of superlatives, younger children will enjoy this book.

Bishop, Clare Huchet

TWENTY AND TEN 1

⌛ WORLD WAR TWO ⊕ FRANCE © 1952

France is occupied by the German army, and twenty children are sent to the mountains for safety. When the children and their caretakers are asked to hide ten Jewish children, they do whatever it takes to keep the children safe.

Blackmore, R. D.

LORNA DOONE 3

⌛ LATE 1600S ⊕ ENGLAND © 1869

John Ridd's father is killed by a marauding band of Doones, forcing John to support his family and their large farm. John discovers a secret way into Doone Valley, where he meets Lorna Doone. As John grows older, he falls in love with Lorna Doone. His love gets him into trouble. At their wedding, John's rival tries to kill Lorna. This is a story of highwaymen, a stolen diamond necklace, and deadly jealousy.

Bond, Michael

A BEAR CALLED PADDINGTON 1

⌛ 1900S 🌐 ENGLAND © 1958

Paddington is a teddy bear found at a London train station with a tag that reads, "Please look after this bear." He claims to come from Darkest Peru and has a great fondness for marmalade. The Brown family loves him, despite the mischief he continually manages to find.

A great read-aloud for younger children, with subtle humor for older children and parents.

Boyd, James

DRUMS 2

⌛ AMERICAN REVOLUTION 🌐 NORTH CAROLINA & ENGLAND © 1925

Johnny Fraser leaves his backwoods home in North Carolina to fight in the Revolutionary War. This is one of my mother's favorites.

Brady, Esther Wood

TOLIVER'S SECRET 1

⌛ 1770S 🌐 NEW ENGLAND © 1976

Disguised as a boy, ten-year-old Ellen Toliver carries a secret message to General Washington. The endeavor seems simple at the start, but the British change their plans, and she finds her way webbed with danger.

Brill, Ethel C.

MADELEINE TAKES COMMAND 1

⌛ 1690S 🌐 FRENCH CANADA © 1946

With her parents away, fourteen-year-old Madeleine de Vercheres and her brothers defend a small outpost against Indian attack.

Brink, Carol Ryrie

CADDIE WOODLAWN 1

⌛ 1860S 🌐 WISCONSIN © 1935

Caddie Woodlawn is the grandmother of the author. This is the story of her adventures in Wisconsin in 1860.

MAGICAL MELONS 1

⌛ 1860S 🌐 WISCONSIN © 1944

A sequel to *Caddie Woodlawn*.

Brontë, Charlotte

JANE EYRE 3

⌛ EARLY 1800S 🌐 ENGLAND © 1847

Jane Eyre tells us the story of her life. She was unloved and abused as a child. When she is old enough, she leaves to be a governess at Thornfield. She falls in love with her employer Mr. Rochester, but when she discovers at their wedding that Rochester is already married, she flees in despair. This is a story of Jane's difficult choices between what she wants and what she believes is right.

Buchan, John

PRESTER JOHN 2

⌛ 1910S 🌐 SCOTLAND & SOUTH AFRICA © 1910

Young Davie Crawfurd has a strange adventure with a huge black man on a seashore of Scotland. Later, he travels to South Africa and again meets that mysterious black man, who leads him into a wild African adventure. This is one of Buchan's best adventure stories.

THE THIRTY-NINE STEPS 2

⌛ 1914 🌐 ENGLAND & SCOTLAND © 1915

After a few months of retired London life, Richard Hannay is completely bored. But things change. He finds a murdered man in his flat *and* is accused of murder *and* is in possession of a vital national secret *and* is wanted by a ring of dangerous spies *and* is chased all over England and Scotland *and* is almost killed I forget how many times.

This is one of the first spy stories ever written. Buchan is one of our family's favorite authors, especially when my mother reads him in dialect.

ADVENTURES OF RICHARD HANNAY 2

⌛ 1910S 🌐 EUROPE © 1915

These three spy stories follow *The Thirty-Nine Steps.* Sometimes we wonder how one person can get into so many jams, and every time Hannay find a friend to help him at the last moment.

SALUTE TO ADVENTURERS 2

⌛ LATE 1600S 🌐 SCOTLAND & VIRGINIA © 1917

Andrew Garvald sails for Virginia to better his prospects. There he finds a wild land where the colonists are in danger from Indians.

Bulwer-Lytton, Sir Edward G.

THE LAST DAYS OF POMPEII 3

⌛ AD 9 🌐 POMPEII, ITALY © 1834

Glaucus is a wealthy Greek living in Pompeii. He falls in love with Ione, the Grecian ward of the Egyptian Arbaces. Arbaces wishes to marry Ione himself and accuses Glaucus of murdering Ione's brother. Glaucus is condemned to die in the arena. At the vital moment Mount Vesuvius erupts, casting the city of Pompeii into panic.

Bunyan, John

THE PILGRIM'S PROGRESS 2

⌛ 1600S 🌐 ENGLAND OR ANYWHERE © 1678

Christian despairs of his life in the City of Destruction. He sets off down the straight and narrow way to the far-off City of Zion. His path is beset with obstacles – like Mr. Worldly Wise, the darts of Apollyon, the lures of Vanity Fair, imprisonment in Doubting Castle, and finally crossing the River of Death.

Long ago, this book and the Bible were the only two books families could afford to keep in their homes.

Burgess, Thornton W.

OLD MOTHER WEST WIND 1

⏳ ANYTIME 🌐 GREEN MEADOWS © 1910

A book of moral stories using animals as characters.

THE ADVENTURES OF JERRY MUSKRAT 1

⏳ ANYTIME 🌐 SMILING POOL © 1914

Moral stories about a muskrat and otter.

Burnett, Frances Hodgson

LITTLE LORD FAUNTLEROY 2

⏳ 1800S 🌐 UNITED STATES & ENGLAND © 1886

Precocious Cedric Errol lives with his mother in America. When he is told he is heir to an English lord, his grandfather, he and his mother move to England.

A LITTLE PRINCESS 1

⏳ LATE 1800S 🌐 LONDON © 1888

Before going to war, Sara Crewe's father placed her in Miss Minchin's Select Seminary for Young Girls. Sara's father dies in India, leaving her an orphan. Miss Minchin forces Sara to become a kitchen maid to pay off her debts.

One of my mother's favorites to read aloud.

THE SECRET GARDEN 1

⏳ LATE 1800S 🌐 INDIA & ENGLAND © 1912

Mary Lennox's parents have died, and she must move from India to live with her humpbacked uncle at Misselthwaite Manor in England. She is angry with everyone about her life. Mary discovers a neglected garden and is captivated with making it live again. Mary's cousin Colin also lives in the house as an invalid. Their melancholy lives change as they discover hope in their hidden garden.

THE LOST PRINCE 1

⏳ LATE 1800S 🌐 LONDON © 1914

Marco Loristan lives in exile with his father, waiting until a secret society can restore them to the Samavian throne. He meets with many adventures among the London slums with the Rat, a crippled street urchin.

Burnford, Sheila

THE INCREDIBLE JOURNEY 1

⌛ 1900S 🌐 CANADA © 1960

A bull terrier, a Labrador retriever, and a Siamese cat travel 250 miles through the Canadian wilderness to return to their home. They stick close to one another, helping each other through the journey.

One of my mother's favorites to read aloud.

Butler, Mildred Allen

TWICE QUEEN OF FRANCE: ANNE OF BRITTANY 2

⌛ 1400S 🌐 FRANCE © 1967

Anne inherits Brittany when her father Francis II dies. She marries King Charles to become queen of France. Charles dies at an early age, and she must marry again.

Carlson, Natalie Savage

THE FAMILY UNDER THE BRIDGE 1

⌛ 1900S 🌐 PARIS © 1958

Armand lives as a hobo under a bridge in Paris. He keeps his possessions in an old baby buggy. He enjoys his self-centered, carefree life until his path crosses a struggling mother and her children. Armand reluctantly gives them a place to live. This is a story of sacrificial love.

Carroll, Lewis (Charles Dodgson)

ALICE'S ADVENTURES IN WONDERLAND 2

⌛ 1800S 🌐 ENGLAND & WONDERLAND © 1865

Alice follows the white rabbit down a hole. She enters a land where she becomes small by drinking liquid, the Cheshire cat disappears at will, flamingos are used for croquet mallets, and the Queen of Hearts sentences Alice to death for not knowing anything.

Logical adults find this tale ridiculous, but it has delighted children ever since it delighted Queen Victoria.

THROUGH THE LOOKING-GLASS 2

⌛ 1800S 🌐 LOOKING-GLASS LAND © 1871

This time Alice goes through to the other side of a mirror. This world is a chess board where Alice must travel to the other side of the board to become a queen herself.

Carroll hid mathematical and logical principles in these stories.

Caudill, Rebecca

TREE OF FREEDOM 1

⌛ 1780 ⊕ KENTUCKY © 1949

Thirteen-year-old Stephanie moves from Carolina to Kentucky to find their new life just as hard. This is a story of character and family survival.

SCHOOLROOM IN THE PARLOR 1

⌛ EARLY 1900S ⊕ KENTUCKY © 1959

The Fairfield children can't go to school in the winter because of the heavy snow. Althy is asked to teach school in the parlor.

THE FAR-OFF LAND 1

⌛ 1780S ⊕ TENNESSEE & KENTUCKY © 1964

Ketty Petrie is an orphan. She leaves the Moravian settlement in North Carolina to travel to her brother out west.

Cleary, Beverly

ELLEN TEBBITS 1

⌛ MID-1900S ⊕ OREGON © 1951

Ellen is excited to have a new friend. She and Austine share adventures until Ellen makes a terrible mistake and their friendship is broken.

EMILY'S RUNAWAY IMAGINATION 1

⌛ EARLY 1900S ⊕ OREGON © 1961

Emily lives on a farm in Oregon. Emily is spunky and imaginative and manages to get into funny situations. The setting and incidents in this book are based on the author's own childhood in the early twentieth century.

RAMONA QUIMBY, AGE 8 1

⌛ LATE 1900S ⊕ AMERICA © 1981

Ramona Quimby has just entered the third grade, and her life has become more complicated. True, she does get to ride the school bus all by herself, but she now has a teacher who thinks she is a nuisance and a classmate who steals her eraser. She tries to solve her problems, but only ends up with egg in her hair.

DEAR MR. HENSHAW 2

⌛ LATE 1900S 🌐 CALIFORNIA © 1983

Leigh Botts writes to his favorite author, Mr. Henshaw, who suggests that Leigh keep a diary. Leigh writes about his plans, his successes, and his troubles at school and at home with a single mother and a father he rarely sees.

Written with sympathy and simplicity, this book helps the reader grow in understanding about people.

Coatsworth, Elizabeth

FIVE BUSHEL FARM 1

⌛ 1700S 🌐 UNITED STATES © 1939

Sally and Andrew help each other build a new home in pioneer country.

Collins, Wilkie

THE WOMAN IN WHITE **3**

⌛ EARLY 1800S ⊕ ENGLAND © 1860

A mysterious woman is confined to an asylum. Why? This story is told though the voice of several characters in the mystery.

THE MOONSTONE **3**

⌛ 1799-1849 ⊕ INDIA & ENGLAND © 1868

The "Moonstone" is a yellow diamond stolen from the forehead of a Hindu moon-god statue in India and eventually inherited by Rachel Verinder. This is the story of how the stone is again stolen and the troubled romance between Rachel and Franklin Blake. If I told you any more, I would spoil the mystery for you.

The story is told from the perspective of several different witnesses to the crime.

Collodi, Carlo

PINOCCHIO **2**

⌛ 1800S ⊕ EUROPE © 1892

Pinocchio is a wooden puppet who is forever getting into trouble, disobeying his master Geppetto, and falling in with bad companions. His nose grows longer every time he lies. In the end, he learns to mend his ways.

Cooper, James Fenimore

THE LAST OF THE MOHICANS **2**

⌛ 1757 ⊕ NEW YORK STATE © 1826

Alice and Cora are on their way to Fort William Henry when they are captured by renegade Huron Indians. They are freed by the brave Hawkeye and his Mohican friends and arrive at the fort just in time for the French to attack.

I remember reading this book myself and not being able to let it out of my hands until I was done.

THE DEERSLAYER **2**

⌛ 1740S ⊕ NEW YORK © 1841

This first of the Leatherstocking Tales shows us Natty Bumppo's early years as a frontiersman and how he meets Judith.

Cornelissen, Cornelia

SOFT RAIN 1

⏳ 1838 ⊕ SOUTHERN AMERICA © 1998

Soft Rain is a nine-year-old Cherokee girl. One day soldiers force Soft Rain and her mother from their home, leaving the rest of their family behind. Along with 18,000 of their people, they make a dangerous journey over mountains to a new home in the west. This is the story of the Trail of Tears of 1838.

Dahlstedt, Marden

THE TERRIBLE WAVE 1

⏳ 1889 ⊕ JOHNSTOWN, PENNSYLVANIA © 1972

Johnstown is washed away by a great wave released when the South Fork Dam breaks. Megan Maxwell learns to be less self-centered and to think of others as she searches for her family.

Dalgliesh, Alice

THE COURAGE OF SARAH NOBLE 1

⏳ 1707 ⊕ CONNECTICUT © 1954

At age eight Sarah Noble travels with her father to build a home in the frontier. She has the courage to deal with the dark woods, wild animals, and Indians.

Day, Clarence

LIFE WITH FATHER 2

⏳ LATE 1800S ⊕ NEW YORK CITY © 1935

Clarence Day, Jr. tells the story of his life with his eccentric father, Clarence Day, Sr. There were times when my family rolled around on the floor in agonies of laughter when Dad read this book to us.

Day, Veronique

LANDSLIDE 1

⏳ MID-1900S ⊕ EUROPE © 1963

Five children are trapped in a house by a landslide. Unfortunately, no one knows they are inside.

de Angeli, Marguerite

THEE, HANNAH! 1

⏳ MID-1800S 🌐 PHILADELPHIA © 1940

Hannah is a Quaker living in Philadelphia before the Civil War. She longs to wear fashionable clothes instead of simple Quaker garb. She comes to appreciate her family's religion when she helps her family save a runaway slave.

THE DOOR IN THE WALL 1

⏳ MIDDLE AGES 🌐 ENGLAND © 1949

Young Robin is crippled by a strange illness. Brother Luke helps Robin out of plague-ridden London and brings him to Sir Peter de Lindsay's castle, where Robin learns to serve as a page. The Lindsay Castle is attacked by a Welsh force, and Robin must go for help.

This book is one of my mother's favorites to read aloud and provides an excellent lesson on overcoming obstacles.

BLACK FOX OF LORNE 1

⏳ AD 900 🌐 SCOTLAND © 1954

Jan and Brus are identical twin brothers. They sail with their family from the crowded Norse country to free land in the British Isles. They are shipwrecked on the Scottish coast and must use their wits and likeness to escape their captors and find their mother again.

Defoe, Daniel

ROBINSON CRUSOE 2

⏳ 1651-1705 🌐 ISLAND OFF SOUTH AMERICA © 1719

Robinson Crusoe's parents want him to settle down in the happy middle station in life, but he rebels and sets out for the sea. He is eventually shipwrecked on a tropical island and uses his ingenuity to survive with plants and animals. Crusoe's loneliness and hardships slowly mature his character. His loneliness ends when he saves a native from being eaten alive by fellow cannibals.

You will appreciate reading an unabridged version of this book.

A JOURNAL OF THE PLAGUE YEAR 2

⧗ 1665 ⊕ LONDON © 1722

This is a fictionalized account of the 1665 plague in London.

De Jong, Meindert

THE WHEEL ON THE SCHOOL 1

⧗ 1800S ⊕ HOLLAND © 1954

Some children put a wheel on their school for the storks to roost upon.

THE HOUSE OF 60 FATHERS 2

⧗ WORLD WAR TWO ⊕ CHINA © 1956

The Japanese burn Tien Pao's village. When Tien Pao is separated from his family, he must scramble though the mountains with his pet pig. He is helped along by fighters in the Chinese resistance. Tien Pao is discovered by two American soldiers and taken to their camp. A bomber squadron decides to adopt Tien Pao, becoming his "House of Sixty Fathers."

The book describes the vivid details of war; use caution with children who may be frightened.

de la Ramée, Louise (Ouida)

A DOG OF FLANDERS 2

⧗ EARLY 1800S ⊕ FLANDERS

Nello finds a cart dog left to die on the road side. The dog recovers and helps Nello and his grandfather carry milk to the village. Nello dreams of learning to paint and seeing the great masterpiece by Rubens hanging in the cathedral, but he has no money. In the end, one of his dreams come true.

de Treviño, Elizabeth Borton

I, JUAN DE PAREJA 2

⧗ 1600S ⊕ SPAIN © 1965

Juan de Pareja is the slave of the painter Velázquez. Juan learns to paint while mixing paints for his master. Slaves in Spain were forbidden to paint, but Velázquez discovers that his slave has talent, and they develop a lifelong friendship. Juan is allowed to paint and becomes a respected artist in his own right.

Dickens, Charles

NICHOLAS NICKLEBY 3

⏳ EARLY 1800S 🌐 ENGLAND © 1838

The story of the Nicklebys and how they overcome poverty.

OLIVER TWIST 2

⏳ 1800S 🌐 ENGLAND © 1839

Oliver Twist runs away from the workhouse. In London he is found by Fagin, the thief-trainer. Fagin sends him to learn pickpocketing from the Artful Dodger. Oliver is caught, though not guilty, and sent to jail. When Mr. Brownlow rescues Oliver, he is recaptured by Fagin and sent with Bill Sikes to burglarize a house.

This is our family's favorite Dickens book to read aloud.

A CHRISTMAS CAROL 2

⏳ 1800S 🌐 ENGLAND © 1843

Ebenezer Scrooge is visited on Christmas Eve by three ghosts who show him his mistakes and offer him an opportunity to change. Scrooge is best remembered for saying, "Bah! Humbug," but he deserves to be remembered for repentance and for taking advantage of an opportunity to live better.

DAVID COPPERFIELD 3

⏳ 1800S 🌐 ENGLAND © 1850

David tells the story of his life. The meandering plot of this book is a setting for the people David meets along the way. And what people they are! Do you want villains? Dickens shows you Mr. Murdstone, Uriah Heep, and Mr. Creakle. Yet with all the evil people, Dickens encourages us with bright stars of good character that shine through David's misfortunes.

BLEAK HOUSE 3

⏳ 1800S 🌐 ENGLAND © 1852

This story centers around the lawcase of Jarndyce and Jarndyce that never ends and Esther Summerson's selfless determination to help the troubled people around her. Considered by some to be Dickens' greatest work, this story weaves some of his most despicable villains among truly honest and funny characters.

LITTLE DORRIT 3

⌛ 1800S 🌐 ENGLAND, FRANCE & ITALY © 1857

Little Dorrit is a young woman with a self-sacrificing heart and sweet disposition. She is devoted to her father, who is in prison for debt. This is also the story of Arthur Clennam and how he tries to help Little Dorrit in the midst of the mystery surrounding him.

A TALE OF TWO CITIES 3

⌛ 1775 🌐 LONDON & FRANCE © 1859

"It was the best of times, it was the worst of times, it was the age of wisdom, it was the age of foolishness, it was the epoch of belief, it was the epoch of incredulity, it was the season of Light, it was the season of Darkness. . . ."

This story begins with the social unrest surrounding the crumbling French monarchy. Characters in this story include the loyal businessman Mr. Lorry; Dr. Manette, who goes insane while unjustly imprisoned in the Bastille; Lucie, Dr. Manette's daughter; Charles Darnay, who renounced his name and fortune as Marquis St. Evrémonde because of what his father and ancestors did to the peasants and who falls in love with Lucie; Sydney Carton, the irresolute genius who is Darnay's look-alike; and Madame Defarge, a woman consumed with revenge for what the former Marquis St. Evrémonde did. This is a story of the French Revolution and its causes.

GREAT EXPECTATIONS 3

⌛ 1800S 🌐 ENGLAND © 1861

Pip is an orphan, raised by his cruel sister and her kind husband Joe. Pip meets the wealthy Miss Havisham and her ward Estella and longs to become prosperous like them. When Pip's wishes are granted by an anonymous benefactor, he must decide who he truly is.

This is my least favorite Dickens story.

OUR MUTUAL FRIEND 3

⌛ 1800S 🌐 LONDON © 1865

Dickens's last completed novel begins with mystery and murder on the Thames River. John Harmon is drowned. We follow various people as they try to gain his fortune. Dickens gives us a picture of the shallowness of wealthy society with its endless dinners and social activities and how, in the end, it cannot appreciate honest character.

Dodge, Mary Mapes

HANS BRINKER, OR THE SILVER SKATES 2

⌛ 1800S 🌐 HOLLAND © 1865

Hans and Gretel long to race in the great race with real skates, not their wooden skates. However, they must work for bread to feed themselves and their father, who is bedridden after a head injury.

Doyle, Arthur Conan

A STUDY IN SCARLET 2

⌛ 1881 🌐 LONDON © 1887

Dr. Watson returns from service in Afghanistan and is introduced to a scientist named Sherlock Holmes. Holmes expresses interest in sharing rooms at 221B Baker Street with him. Holmes remains a perfect enigma to Watson until Holmes takes him into his confidence and lets Watson tag along as Holmes solves a mystery that has baffled Scotland Yard.

This story introduced the character who, from 1887 until Doyle's death in 1930, dominated mystery fiction and serves as the example of the perfect detective. These short stories and novels are considered the best examples of Victorian English literary development.

THE SIGN OF THE FOUR 2

⌛ 1888 🌐 LONDON © 1890

Sherlock Holmes is exhausted by boredom, but he is revived again when he and Watson search for a fabulous Indian treasure and the murderer of one of its owners. While unraveling a tangle of clues, Dr. Watson finds himself in love with Mary Morstan, the woman who brought Holmes the mystery. The most exciting of Doyle's four novels, this story will leave you thirsting for more and more and more.

THE ADVENTURES OF SHERLOCK HOLMES **2**

⌛ LATE 1800S 🌐 ENGLAND © 1892

This collection contains "A Scandal in Bohemia," "The Red-Headed League," "A Case of Identity," "The Boscombe Valley Mystery," "The Five Orange Pips," "The Man with the Twisted Lip," "The Adventure of the Blue Carbuncle," "The Adventure of the Speckled Band," "The Adventure of the Engineer's Thumb," "The Adventure of the Noble Bachelor," "The Adventure of the Beryl Coronet," and "The Adventure of the Copper Beeches."

THE MEMOIRS OF SHERLOCK HOLMES **2**

⌛ LATE 1800S 🌐 ENGLAND © 1894

This collection contains "The Adventure of Silver Blaze," "The Adventure of the Cardboard Box," "The Adventure of the Yellow Face," "The Adventure of the Stockbroker's Clerk," "The Adventure of the Gloria Scott," "The Adventure of the Musgrave Ritual," "The Adventure of the Reigate Squire," "The Adventure of the Crooked Man," "The Adventure of the Resident Patient," "The Adventure of the Greek Interpreter," "The Adventure of the Naval Treaty," and "The Adventure of the Final Problem."

THE HOUND OF THE BASKERVILLES **2**

⌛ LATE 1800S 🌐 LONDON & DARTMOOR © 1902

Sherlock Holmes and Watson are called to investigate a ghost dog that haunts the moor around the house of the Baskervilles.

THE RETURN OF SHERLOCK HOLMES **2**

⌛ LATE 1800S 🌐 ENGLAND © 1904

This collection contains "The Adventure of the Empty House," "The Adventure of the Norwood Builder," "The Adventure of the Dancing Men," "The Adventure of the Solitary Cyclist," "The Adventure of the Priory School," "The Adventure of Black Peter," "The Adventure of Charles Augustus Milverton," "The Adventure of the Six Napoleons," "The Adventure of the Three Students," "The Adventure of the Golden Pince-Nez," "The Adventure of the Missing Three-Quarter," "The Adventure of the Abbey Grange," and "The Adventure of the Second Stain."

THE LOST WORLD 2

⌛ EARLY 1900S ⊕ LONDON & SOUTH AMERICA
© 1912

Professor Challenger leads an expedition to the Amazon jungle in search of a land where dinosaurs and ape-men live. This is one of our favorite Doyle stories.

THE VALLEY OF FEAR

⌛ LATE 1800S ⊕ LONDON & UNITED STATES © 1914

A mining town in America is controlled by terror. Holmes must solve an impossible murder in a castle house and bring peace to an old fear.

HIS LAST BOW

⌛ LATE 1800S ⊕ ENGLAND © 1917

This collection contains "The Adventure of Wisteria Lodge," "The Adventure of the Cardboard Box," "The Adventure of the Red Circle," "The Adventure of the Bruce-Partington Plans," "The Adventure of the Dying Detective," "The Disappearance of Lady Frances Carfax," "The Adventure of the Devil's Foot," and "His Last Bow."

THE WHITE COMPANY 3

⌛ 1360S ⊕ ENGLAND & FRANCE © 1922

Alleyne Edricson sets out in search of adventure and finds it as Sir Nigel Corning's squire. Sir Nigel is making his way to France to join the White Company. Along the way, Alleyne is entangled in jousts, skirmishes, and a daring rescue from a besieged castle.

Doyle considered this his greatest work, but we thought it was somewhat dry.

THE CASE-BOOK OF SHERLOCK HOLMES

⌛ LATE 1800S ⊕ ENGLAND © 1927

This collection contains "The Adventure of the Mazarin Stone," "The Problem of Thor Bridge," "The Adventure of the Creeping Man," "The Adventure of the Sussex Vampire," "The Adventure of the Three Garridebs," "The Adventure of the Illustrious Client," "The Adventure of the Three Gables," "The Adventure of the Blanched Soldier," "The Adventure of the Lion's Mane," "The Adventure of the Retired Colourman," "The Adventure of the Veiled Lodger," and "The Adventure of Shoscombe Old Place."

du Bois, William Pène

THE TWENTY-ONE BALLOONS 1

⌛ 1880s 🌐 BALLOON & KRAKATOA © 1947

Professor William Waterman Sherman plans to enjoy his retirement by taking a balloon trip alone around the globe. While over the ocean, a seagull punctures his balloon, and the professor is marooned on the island of Krakatoa. He discovers the island is inhabited by several very rich European families who have changed their names to a single letter of the alphabet. When Mr. F shows the professor the sparkling secret created by the island's volcanic crater, the professor realizes they will never let him leave.

This book is one of my mother's favorites to read aloud, and it deserved its Newbery Award.

Eckert, Allan W.

INCIDENT AT HAWK'S HILL 1

⌛ 1870's 🌐 DAKOTAS © 1971

A shy boy named Ben wanders off from his family into the tall prairie grass. After searching for two days, his family is told he is dead. But Ben has taken shelter in a hole and has been adopted by a female badger. His brother finds Ben in time to save him from malnutrition. The MacDonald family accepts the badger because she kept Ben alive.

Edmonds, Walter

THE MATCHLOCK GUN 1

⌛ 1757 🌐 ALBANY, NEW YORK © 1941

When their father leaves to fight the Indians and the French, Edward and Trudy and their mother are left alone. They notice smoke in the distance, and Edward's mother takes down the old Spanish gun from over the fireplace and loads it. She sets it up on a table and shows Edward how to fire it. Then she leaves to check for Indians.

This is one of the most classic stories for young children. Even older children can appreciate the danger and courage in this story.

TOM WHIPPLE 1

⌛ 1800S ⊕ AMERICA & RUSSIA © 1942

This is a humorous tale of a Yankee boy who sails to Russia carrying a present for the czar.

TWO LOGS CROSSING: JOHN HASKELL'S STORY 1

⌛ PIONEER TIMES ⊕ ADIRONDACK MOUNTAINS © 1943

John Haskell's father dies, and John must support his family and repay his father's debts.

CADMUS HENRY 2

⌛ CIVIL WAR ⊕ AMERICA © 1949

The story of a Confederate aeronaut in the Civil War.

Eggleston, Edward

THE HOOSIER SCHOOLMASTER 2

⌛ 1800S ⊕ INDIANA © 1871

A schoolmaster begins his first year teaching in an Indiana community. This book is famous for its use of regional dialect. Chapters like "Spelling down the Master" describe a typical spelling school.

Eliot, George (Mary Ann Evans)

SILAS MARNER 3

⌛ EARLY 1800S ⊕ ENGLAND © 1861

Every night Silas Marner counts his gold, and all day he weaves cloth to sell for more gold. One day he finds his gold has been stolen, and he is broken with grief. Days later, Silas finds a little girl with golden hair sleeping on his fireplace. He adopts the little girl. Raising her teaches him not to mourn the loss of his gold.

George Eliot shows how wrong it is to ignore your past, but if you invest in good things, you will be forgiven.

Ellis, Mel

SAD SONG OF THE COYOTE 1

⌛ EARLY 1900S ⊕ WISCONSIN © 1967

A boy hunts coyotes to pay for college. He finds a litter of orphaned coyotes.

IRONHEAD 1

⌛ 1900S ⊕ FLORIDA EVERGLADES © 1970

A terrible experience has made Doug's father mentally ill. Doug supports the family by catching rattlesnakes to extract the venom used in antidotes. He dreams of catching a legendary rattler and using the money to obtain treatment for his father. This story shows how danger can make people do amazing things.

Estes, Eleanor

THE MIDDLE MOFFAT 1

⌛ EARLY 1900S ⊕ CONNECTICUT © 1942

Ten-year-old Jane Moffat is the middle child in her family. She has many adventures in their small Connecticut town.

THE HUNDRED DRESSES 1

⌛ MID-1900S ⊕ UNITED STATES © 1944

Wanda Petronski wears the same dress to school every day. Her classmates tease and isolate her. One day, she claims that she has a hundred dresses at home.

GINGER PYE 1

⌛ 1900 ⊕ UNITED STATES © 1951

Ginger is a pet puppy bought by Jerry and Rachel Pye. Ginger disappears one day, and the children suspect a stranger with a yellow hat. This is a book filled with funny characters.

Falk, Elsa

WINTER JOURNEY 1

⌛ 1800S ⊕ AMERICA © 1955

Chris Arp brings his family though the winter wilderness to Minnesota Territory.

Farley, Walter

THE BLACK STALLION 1

⌛ MID-1900S ⊕ DESERT ISLAND & UNITED STATES © 1944

Alec Ramsay and a black Arabian stallion are shipwrecked on a island. Alec tames The Black and rides him bareback. They are rescued and brought home to the United States. Alec's neighbor takes an interest in the horse and teaches Alec to race The Black.

Obviously very popular, this story is good to read aloud.

Ferris, Helen

FAVORITE POEMS OLD AND NEW 1

⌛ ALL ⊕ EVERYWHERE © 1957

Helen Ferris begins this collection by describing the special role poetry had in her childhood. Her selection of poems will enrich children's lives.

Field, Elsie Kimmell

PRAIRIE WINTER 1

⌛ 1800S ⊕ MIDWEST AMERICA © 1959

Mr. Kimmell draws a winning number in the lottery for land in South Dakota. Mrs. Kimmell and their children stay on their new land during the winter as Mr. Kimmell returns to Iowa to earn money.

Field, Rachel

HITTY: HER FIRST HUNDRED YEARS 1

⌛ 1800-1900S ⊕ ALL OVER THE WORLD © 1929

Hitty is a doll made for Phoebe Prible from a piece of well-seasoned mountain ash wood. Hitty tells the story of her first hundred years and how she is owned by many little girls, is lost several times, and sees many changes take place in society over her lifetime. By the end, we wonder if she will have even more adventures.

One of my mother's favorites to read aloud.

CALICO BUSH 2

⌛ MID-1700S ⊕ MAINE © 1931

Marguerite Ledoux comes to the New World indentured to serve a family in the wilderness of Maine.

HEPATICA HAWKS 1

⌛ EARLY 1900S ⊕ AMERICA © 1932

Hepatica is so tall she is part of a circus freak show.

Fisher, Dorothy Canfield

UNDERSTOOD BETSY 1

⌛ 1800S ⊕ VERMONT © 1917

Elizabeth Ann moves from her sheltered city home to life in the country. This is the story of how she grows into a healthier, happier girl.

Fleming, Ian

CHITTY CHITTY BANG BANG 1

⌛ MID-1900S ⊕ ENGLAND & FRANCE © 1964

The big green Paragon Panther has a license plate that reads, "GEN11." Mr. Pott finds the car in a junkyard and fixes it up for his family. At first, the car won't start. When it does start, it says "Chitty . . . Chitty . . . Bang-Bang." The Potts discover their car can drive very fast and transform itself into an aeroplane and a speed boat! The Pott family flies to an island in the English channel for a picnic. There they discover a gangster's hidden cave. This is the humorous story of a car with a mind of its own.

Forbes, Esther

JOHNNY TREMAIN 1

⌛ 1775-1776 ⊕ BOSTON © 1943

Johnny Tremain is an orphan, apprenticed to Mr. Lapham, a Boston silversmith. Johnny bullies the other apprentices. Johnny's hand is badly burned by molten silver, and when the bandage is removed, the hand has not healed well. Now Johnny cannot work as a silversmith, and instead he carries messages for the Committee of Public Safety. His greatest desire is to regain the use of his hand so he can hold a musket and fight for independence. This is a story of the American Revolution before Lexington Green.

Fox, Mary Virginia

TREASURE OF THE REVOLUTION 1

⌛ AMERICAN REVOLUTION ⊕ AMERICA © 1961

A brother and sister must carry a treasure from Philadelphia to Virginia during the American Revolution.

French, Allen

THE STORY OF ROLF AND THE VIKING BOW 2

⌛ AD 1010 🌐 ICELAND & BRITISH ORKNEYS © 1900

Rolf is the son of Hiarandi the Unlucky – so named because of misfortunes that come on him after he lights a fire-beacon on the coastland cliff. He lights the beacon because he believes it to be a good Christian thing to warn ships of danger. Hiarandi is banished to his farm for a year because he cannot recompense a wrong done by his evil brother. When Hiarandi accidentally strays over the boundary of his farm, he is murdered by Einar. Rolf must prove that his father was not rightly killed by shooting an arrow beyond the spot of the murder.

This story gives a wonderful feeling for what life was like in Iceland in the early second millennium AD.

THE COLONIALS 3

⌛ 1772 🌐 MICHIGAN & BOSTON © 1902

Francis Ellery rescues Alice from the Indians. Meanwhile, war brews in Boston.

This is one of my mother's favorite books to read aloud.

LOST BARON: A STORY OF ENGLAND IN THE YEAR 1200 2

⌛ 1200S 🌐 ENGLAND © 1940

Martin is Baron Eric's page. His life abruptly changes when the baron disappears and Sir Basil takes charge of the castle.

THE RED KEEP: A STORY OF BURGUNDY IN 1165 2

⌛ 1165 🌐 FRANCE © 1939

The Sauval brothers terrorize the surrounding lands to bring everything under their control. Sir Roger and Conan must stop them from taking the Red Keep.

Fritz, Jean

THE CABIN FACED WEST 1

⌛ LATE 1700S 🌐 PENNSYLVANIA © 1958

Ann Hamilton works with her family building a new farm in western Pennsylvania. She longs for something exciting to happen. Her mother's twelve china plates wait for a special occasion, which comes as a surprise to everyone. This quick-moving story is based on events in the life of the author's ancestors.

Gaskell, Elizabeth

NORTH AND SOUTH 3

⌛ 1800S 🌐 ENGLAND © 1855

Margaret Hale's family must move from their beloved home in the south of England to the bleak, industrial north. Margaret fights for social justice and comes head-to-head with John Thornton, a mill owner. Her thinking expands through her adversities. She must learn to admit her mistakes. This story uses narrative to describe facts about social issues of the time.

WIVES AND DAUGHTERS 3

⌛ 1800S 🌐 ENGLAND © 1866

Molly is devoted to her father and is happy in the simple pleasures of their life. When her father suddenly remarries, her new stepmother and stepsister make Molly's life confusing. This story combines a compelling plot with a warm understanding of how people think.

Gipson, Fred

OLD YELLER 1

⌛ 1860S 🌐 TEXAS © 1956

When his father drives the cattle to Abilene, Travis is the man of the house. Travis finds a stray dog eating a side of their pork, and he tries to beat it off. But Travis's little brother Arliss won't let him. They name the dog Old Yeller. The dog proves himself by saving Arliss from an angry bear and Travis from the wild pigs and Ma from the attack of a rabid wolf.

This is one of our family's favorite books.

Goldsmith, Oliver

GOODY TWO-SHOES 2

⌛ 1700S 🌐 ENGLAND © 1765

Margery Meanwell is an orphan with only one shoe.

THE VICAR OF WAKEFIELD 3

⌛ 1700S ⊕ ENGLAND © 1766

Dr. Primrose loses his fortune and must move with his family to a new parish.

Grahame, Kenneth

THE WIND IN THE WILLOWS 1

⌛ EARLY 1900S ⊕ ENGLAND © 1908

These are the adventures of Mole and Rat with Badger, their wise counselor. They spend most of their time rescuing Toad, their conceited, reckless, and charming friend. We sympathize with Mole and Rat, respect old Badger, and feel sorry for selfish Toad and his motorcars.

Rich with humor, *The Wind in the Willows* is for every person of every age.

THE RELUCTANT DRAGON 1

⌛ MIDDLE AGES ⊕ ENGLAND © 1898

A boy finds a dragon in a cave on the Downs. He must convince the village and St. George that it is a peaceful dragon.

Gray, Elizabeth Janet

ADAM OF THE ROAD 1

⌛ 1290S ⊕ ENGLAND © 1942

Adam is a minstrel who wanders the English countryside with his dog, searching for his father.

Grimm, Jacob and Wilhelm

GRIMM'S FAIRY TALES 2

⌛ PAST 🌐 EUROPE © 1812, 1815

Brothers Jacob and Wilhelm Grimm compiled stories from their native northern Europe. We have these brothers to thank for "Sleeping Beauty," "Rumpelstiltskin," "Hansel and Gretel," "Snow White," and "Cinderella." Be aware as you read aloud that some fairy tales are surprisingly frightening.

Haggard, Rider

KING SOLOMON'S MINES

⌛ 1800S 🌐 AFRICA © 1885

Allan Quatermain is asked to explore the interior of Africa in search of the fabled King Solomon's Mines. His party is accompanied by Umbopa, a tall, mysterious African.

Hale, Edward Everett

THE MAN WITHOUT A COUNTRY 2

⌛ 1800S 🌐 AROUND THE WORLD © 1863

During his 1807 court martial, Philip Nolan renounces the United States in a fit of anger. His punishment is to live as a prisoner in naval ships for the remainder of his life, never seeing or hearing of the United States.

This story was published during the Civil War to inspire patriotism.

Harris, Joel Chandler

UNCLE REMUS: HIS SONGS & HIS SAYINGS 1

⌛ 1800S 🌐 GEORGIA © 1880

Uncle Remus tells stories of Brer Rabbit, Brer Fox, and their friends and enemies. Silly, funny, and unexpected, these stories should be read aloud in their wonderful Southern dialect.

Haskell, Helen Eggleston

KATRINKA: THE STORY OF A RUSSIAN CHILD 1

⌛ 1800S 🌐 RUSSIA © 1915

"The story of a little girl who danced her way to her hearts desire."

Havighurst, Walter

SONG OF THE PINES: A STORY OF NORWEGIAN LUMBERING IN WISCONSIN 1

⌛ 1800S ⊕ NORWAY & AMERICA © 1949

Nils Thorsen emigrates from Norway to America, where he teaches lumbermen in Wisconsin to use cant hooks.

Hawes, Charles

THE MUTINEERS 2

⌛ 1700S ⊕ SEA © 1919

Ben Lathrop decides to "follow the sea" and embarks from Massachusetts to China in a ship captained by a friend of his father.

THE DARK FRIGATE 2

⌛ MID-1600S ⊕ ENGLAND © 1923

Philip Marsham's ship *Rose of Devon* is captured by a "gentleman of fortune." Philip accompanies these pirates on their murderous expeditions. The pirates are captured, and Philip is put on trial.

Hawthorne, Nathaniel

TWICE-TOLD TALES 2

⌛ ANCIENT TIME ⊕ ANCIENT LANDS © 1837

A collection of short stories like those in *A Wonder Book.*

THE SCARLET LETTER 3

⌛ 1600S ⊕ MASSACHUSETTS © 1850

This story explores the issues of adultery and integrity. Hester Prynne bears a child by an unknown man, but she refuses to reveal the identity of the child's father. Her Puritan community shuns her as a punishment. Will the father have the honor to come forward himself?

THE HOUSE OF THE SEVEN GABLES 3

⌛ 1700S & 1850 ⊕ SALEM, MASSACHUSETTS © 1851

The wealthy family who built the House of the Seven Gables had the real owner of the property falsely hanged for witchcraft. Before dying, he put a curse on the house. This story concerns how the curse is expiated by the marriage of members from both families.

A WONDER BOOK 2

⏳ ANCIENT TIME 🌐 ANCIENT LANDS © 1852

Eustace Bright tells ancient stories to his cousins, including "The Gorgon's Head," "The Golden Touch," "The Paradise of Children," "The Three Golden Apples," "The Miraculous Pitcher," and "The Chimaera." Children learn the meaning of expressions like "you're opening a Pandora's box" and "he has the golden touch."

TANGLEWOOD TALES 2

⏳ ANCIENT TIME 🌐 ANCIENT LANDS © 1853

A collection of short stories like those in *A Wonder Book*.

Heatter, Basil

WRECK ASHORE 1

⏳ MID-1700S 🌐 FLORIDA © 1969

Matt and his Uncle Nat search for treasure in the Florida Keys.

Herriot, James

ALL CREATURES GREAT AND SMALL 3

⏳ 1930S 🌐 ENGLAND © 1972

Fresh out of vet school, Herriot takes a job helping a Yorkshire veterinarian. In each chapter, Herriot recalls a story of trying to do surgery on a pig before it does surgery on him, or delivering a calf in the cold while the farmer criticizes the new techniques, or convincing a rich old lady to stop feeding her dog fatty food. Out of all the blood and mud, anger and ignorance, Herriot extracts humor and poignant values.

These stories are for mature readers; Herriot records the spicy language of English farmers in unedited form.

Henry, Marguerite

MISTY OF CHINCOTEAGUE 1

⌛ MID-1900S 🌐 CHINCOTEAGUE ISLAND © 1947

Paul and Maureen Beebe have always wanted a pony for themselves. Finally their grandparents let them choose Misty, a horse with a map of the United States on her side. Misty was taken, along with her wild mother, in the yearly roundup of horses on Assateague. The Beebes raise the foal after her mother runs back to the wild. This is a classic tale of sandy life and the wild Spanish horses.

KING OF THE WIND 1

⌛ 1700S 🌐 MOROCCO & EUROPE © 1948

Agba is a mute Arabian boy sent to courier an Arabian stallion that the Sultan of Morocco sends to the King of France. The horse is not recognized as a racer until he and his boy endure hardship and rejection. The Godolphin Arabian becomes a foundation sire of the Thoroughbred line.

SEA STAR, ORPHAN OF CHINCOTEAGUE 1

⌛ 1900S 🌐 NORTH CAROLINA © 1949

In this sequel to *Misty of Chincoteague*, Paul and Maureen find an orphan foal on the beach.

BORN TO TROT 1

⌛ MID-1900S 🌐 KENTUCKY © 1950

Gibson dreams of owning a champion racing horse and winning the Hambletonian. But between school and horses, Gibson has been working too hard. His health is suffering, and his doctor orders a rest.

JUSTIN MORGAN HAD A HORSE 1

⌛ 1800S 🌐 VERMONT © 1954

Joel travels with his schoolteacher, Justin Morgan, to get a horse from a friend. Nobody thinks much of "Little Bub," except Joel. Joel knows the strong little horse has something special in him. Joel sets his heart on buying Little Bub for himself.

STORMY, MISTY'S FOAL 1

⌛ MID-1900S 🌐 CHINCOTEAGUE ISLAND © 1963

The island of Chincoteague experiences a terrible storm that floods the land. The Beebes worry about the horses on Assateague and about Misty, who is about to give birth to her first foal.

Henry, O. (William Sydney Porter)

STORIES 2

⌛ 1800-1900S 🌐 AMERICA © 1884-1910

O. Henry wrote some of the greatest short stories ever written. "The Gift of the Magi" tells how a husband and wife sacrifice what is most dear to buy a present for each other. "The Ransom of Red Chief" tells how a pair of soft-hearted crooks kidnap a redheaded kid who gives them more trouble than they can handle. "A Retrieved Reformation" tells how Jimmy Valentine uses his famed safe-breaking skill to do good. O. Henry is famous for his surprise endings.

Some stories may sail over the head of young children, but most are very much at their level.

Henty, G. A.

ST. GEORGE FOR ENGLAND 1

⌛ 1300S 🌐 ENGLAND © 1885

This is a fictionalized account of the reign of Edward III and the Hundred Years' War, the destruction of the Spanish fleet, the Black Death, and the Jacquerie rising.

BY PIKE AND DYKE 1

⌛ 1570S 🌐 HOLLAND © 1890

This is a fictionalized account of how Holland won independence from Spain.

BY RIGHT OF CONQUEST 1

⌛ 1500S 🌐 MEXICO © 1892

This is a fictionalized account of Hernando Cortez 's conquest of the Aztec Empire.

CAT OF THE BUBASTES 1

⌛ 1250 BC 🌐 EGYPT © 1889

An Egyptian boy accidentally kills a sacred cat and must flee.

...rdahl, Thor

...-TIKI: ACROSS THE PACIFIC BY RAFT 2

⌛ MID-1900S 🌐 FROM PERU TO TAHITI © 1950

Thor Heyerdahl and several friends sail on a balsa wood raft from South America to Tahiti. They want to prove the natives of the Polynesian islands could have sailed in this way, as their ancient legends tell. The raft encounters many dangers on the 101-day journey. This story may inspire children to do something crazy like this.

Hilton, James

GOOD-BYE MR. CHIPS 2

⌛ LATE 1800S–EARLY 1900S 🌐 ENGLAND © 1934

Mr. Chips is a revered fixture at Brookfield School, where he has taught for decades. His dedication to his students, their dedication to him, and his happy marriage makes a humorous and touching story.

Hoff, Carol

HEAD TO THE WEST 1

⌛ 1800S 🌐 TEXAS © 1957

Rosa and Franz move with their parents to Texas in 1840.

Holm, Anne

NORTH TO FREEDOM 1

⌛ MID-1900S 🌐 EUROPE © 1963

Twelve-year-old David has lived in a prison camp all his life. Suddenly he is presented with a chance to escape. He travels through Italy, Switzerland, France, and into Denmark. He discovers everyday things about life that were denied to him in prison.

This book is good for reading aloud and will open a child's eyes to things we take for granted.

Hope, Anthony

THE PRISONER OF ZENDA 3

⌛ 1880S 🌐 EUROPE © 1894

Rudolf Rassendyll has been told that he bears a striking resemblance to the Elphbergs, the ruling family of Ruritania. Rudolf decides to attend the coronation of the new Ruritanian king. He discovers that the likeness is indeed perfect. When the king is kidnapped by the Duke, Rudolf is asked to impersonate the king. Rudolf falls in love with the princess, who was to marry the real king, and the princess falls in love with Rudolf – although she does not know his real identity.

If you like adventure romances, this is a classic.

Howells, William Dean

THE RISE OF SILAS LAPHAM 3

⌛ 1800S 🌐 NEW ENGLAND © 1885

Silas Lapham has become rich. This is the story of how he and his wife and two daughters adjust to life in fashionable society. Their occasional social blunders fill this book with funny situations.

Hughes, Thomas

TOM BROWN'S SCHOOL DAYS 2

⌛ EARLY 1800S 🌐 ENGLAND © 1857

Tom Brown is sent to Rugby, the famous boy's school. He slowly works up the pecking order. Tom and his friends break Flashman, the top bully, of his hold over the younger boys. This story describes life in boarding school and the rewards of remaining stalwartly on the side of right against wrong.

Hugo, Victor

LES MISÉRABLES 3

⌛ 1815-1835 🌐 FRANCE © 1882

Jean Valjean is imprisoned for nine years for stealing a loaf of bread. This is the story of his journey from bitterly hating God to a slow awakening and a desire to do good. Jean Valjean buys the little girl Cosette from the Thénardiers and gives her a happy life as his daughter. But they are followed throughout the story by an unrelenting police detective, Javert, who believes he must bring Jean Valjean to justice. We are shown the slow growth of Valjean's character, interwoven with escapes and battles. The story is besprinkled with glimpses of many wonderful and not-so-wonderful people.

, is truly one of the greatest books ever .en.

Hunt, Irene

ACROSS FIVE APRILS 1

⌛ CIVIL WAR 🌐 ILLINOIS © 1964

Jethro is nine when the Civil War breaks out. His family farms in southern Illinois. One of Jethro's brothers fights in the Union army, while another fights for the Confederacy. Jethro's family is terrorized by cruel townspeople who consider their Southern-sympathizing son a traitor. During the five Aprils of the war, Jethro must shoulder a man's responsibility and learn to cope with a frightening world.

UP A ROAD SLOWLY 1

⌛ EARLY 1900S 🌐 VIRGINIA © 1966

Julie's mother dies, and she must live with her stern aunt Cordelia. Julie's life from age seven to seventeen contains many trials.

Hunt, Mabel Leigh

LUCINDA, A LITTLE GIRL OF 1860 1

⌛ 1860S 🌐 INDIANA © 1934

This is a story of a Quaker girl in Indiana during the Civil War.

Hurnard, Hannah

HINDS' FEET ON HIGH PLACES 2

⌛ FANTASY TIME 🌐 HIGH PLACES © 1955

Written in the style of *The Pilgrim's Progress*, this is an allegorical story of Much-Afraid and her journey with Sorrow and Suffering toward the High Places. She faces many dangers, fears, and setbacks. This book will stimulate good discussions.

Irving, Washington

THE LEGEND OF SLEEPY HOLLOW 2

⌛ 1700S 🌐 AMERICA © 1820

Lanky schoolmaster Ichabod Crane is courting Katrina Van Tassel, the daughter of a prosperous farmer. But her other suitor, the husky, intimidating Brom Bones, disapproves. This is a fun tale.

RIP VAN WINKLE 2

⏳ 1700S 🌐 AMERICA © 1820

Rip Van Winkle is a lazy man, liked by everyone except his wife. One afternoon, he walks into the mountains with his dog Wolf and does not return for twenty years. What happened to Rip Van Winkle in the mountains, and what was he doing all that time?

THE ALHAMBRA 2

⏳ 1600S 🌐 SPAIN © 1832

Peregil is a poor water carrier. A dying Moor gives him a strange box that is the key to a hidden treasure, under the Alhambra. This is the fantastic tale of magic incantations, hidden treasure and traitorous greed.

James, Will

SMOKY THE COWHORSE 1

⏳ 1900S 🌐 WESTERN AMERICA © 1927

Clint the cowboy tells how he fought and broke his wild horse, Smoky. This is the story of their adventures rounding up cattle.

Jeffries, Roderic

TRAPPED 1

⏳ 1900S 🌐 AMERICA © 1972

The river patrol searches for two boys trapped in the mud flats.

Justus, May

THE OTHER SIDE OF THE MOUNTAIN 1

⏳ EARLY 1900S 🌐 TENNESSEE © 1931

Glory lives in a cabin with her widowed mother, grandfather, and brother. She finally is allowed to attend school, but she must travel three miles down the mountain to get to there.

MARY ELLEN 1

⏳ EARLY 1900S 🌐 TENNESSEE © 1947

Mary Ellen lives in a cabin with her family in the Tennessee mountains. The preacher brings a message that Mary Ellen's grandmother wants someone to live with her. Now Mary Ellen has the opportunity to attend school, go to parties and the fair, and learn to quilt and cook. This cheerful story tells about life among the Appalachian mountains.

Keith, Harold

RIFLES FOR WATIE 2

⌛ 1861-65 ⊕ KANSAS, MISSOURI & ARKANSAS
© 1957

Jeff Bussey is a Union infantry soldier in the Civil War. As a spy behind enemy lines, he learns that the rebels are fighting for a cause just as noble as the North.

This story describes a different viewpoint than commonly accepted.

KOMANTCIA 2

⌛ 1860S ⊕ SOUTHWEST AMERICA © 1965

Pedro Pavón, a wealthy Spanish aristocrat, has been banished to his uncle's ranch in northern Mexico. The ranch is raided by Comanches, and only he and his brother Roberto survive. Pedro is made a slave and treated cruelly by his Indian master. Eventually another warrior purchases Pedro and adopts him as a son. Despite his pride and hate for the Indian way of life, Pedro becomes assimilated into their society.

Kelly, Eric P.

THE TRUMPETER OF KRAKOW 2

⌛ 1400S ⊕ POLAND © 1928

Andrew Charnetski has been asked to bringing the Great Tarnov Crystal to the king in Kraków. He hides the crystal in an old pumpkin and journeys to Kraków. Andrew is hired as the night trumpeter in the Church of Our Lady St. Mary and plays the Hejnał each hour. Many people are trying to find the crystal. One is an alchemist who thinks the crystal will help him turn lead into gold. Peter of the Button Face is also looking for the crystal.

I remember my mother reading this story when I was very young. This is one of my favorites.

Kipling, Rudyard

CAPTAINS COURAGEOUS 3

⌛ 1890S ⊕ NEWFOUNDLAND SEA © 1897

Harvey Cheyne is the spoiled son of a millionaire. While on an ocean liner, Harvey is swept overboard. He is rescued by the fishing schooner *We're Here*. The captain does not believe Harvey's story and puts him to work instead of bringing him back to shore. Harvey learns to work with his hands and gains the respect of the fisherman.

THE JUNGLE BOOK 1

⌛ ANCIENT TIME ⊕ INDIA © 1897

Mowgli is a man cub who is raised in the jungle by the animals. They teach him to speak their language. He has many adventures with his friends and is even kidnapped by the silly monkeys. These are classic stories to read aloud to children at bedtime.

KIM 3

⌛ LATE 1800S ⊕ INDIA © 1901

Kim is an orphan raised by a poor Indian woman. Kim leaves his home and follows a llama, hoping he'll find adventure. He is befriended by members of his father's former regiment and sent to school, but not before he proves himself useful to the army by delivering a secret message to a British officer. When Kim gets out of school, he again follows his llama to look for sacred river. Again Kim helps the British Secret Service in India.

JUST SO STORIES 1

⌛ ANCIENT TIME ⊕ INDIA © 1902

The story of how the leopard got his spots, how the elephant stretched his nose, et cetera.

Kjelgaard, Jim

BIG RED 1

⌛ 1900S ⊕ WESTERN AMERICA © 1945

Danny and Big Red roam the Wintapi wilderness hunting Old Majesty, a bear that has wreaked havoc among the cattle ranchers.

IRISH RED 1

⌛ 1900S ⊕ WESTERN AMERICA © 1951

The runt offspring of Big Red seems worthless as a puppy but turns into a champion like his father.

OUTLAW RED 1

⌛ 1900S ⊕ WESTERN AMERICA © 1953

Sean, son of Big Red, runs away from his kennel and must learn to survive on his own.

Kochenderfer, Lee

THE VICTORY GARDEN 1

⌛ WORLD WAR TWO ⊕ KANSAS © 2002

Teresa and her father are Victory gardeners during World War Two. They have a rivalry with their grouchy neighbor. When their neighbor is hospitalized, Teresa organizes her friends to care of his garden. They cooperate in their efforts for the home front.

Knight, Eric

LASSIE COME-HOME 1

⌛ EARLY 1900S ⊕ ENGLAND © 1940

Because Joe's family needs money, Joe must sell his collie to a man in Scotland. Lassie's heart is broken, and the dog runs back to her boy. The hundred-mile journey is fraught with danger.

This book is one of my mother's favorites to read aloud.

Kyle, Elizabeth

THE STORY OF GRIZEL 1

⌛ 1600S ⊕ SCOTLAND & HOLLAND © 1961

Lady Grizel Bailie is a Covenanter Presbyterian. She helps her father escape from capture.

Lamb, Charles and Mary

TALES FROM SHAKESPEARE 1

⌛ ANCIENT & MEDIEVAL TIME ⊕ EUROPE © 1807

Shakespeare's plays are rewritten for children. These include: "The Tempest;" "A Midsummer Night's Dream;" "The Winter's Tale;" "Much Ado about Nothing;" "As You Like It;" "The Two Gentlemen of Verona;" "The Merchant of Venice;" "Cymbeline;" "King Lear;" "Macbeth;" "All's Well That Ends Well;" "The Taming of the Shrew;" "The Comedy of Errors;" "Measure for Measure;" "Twelfth Night;" "Timon of Athens;" "Romeo and Juliet;" "Hamlet, Prince of Denmark;" "Othello;" and "Pericles, Prince of Tyre."

L'Amour, Louis

COLLECTED SHORT STORIES OF LOUIS L'AMOUR 3

⌛ 1800S 🌐 WESTERN AMERICA © 2004

Tough guys with hard fists and quick guns, gutsy women with grey eyes who know what they want, corrupt sheriffs and scheming ranchers with scars in prominent places – all these stories end with a lesson learned, gunfight, and usually a kiss.

Landon, Margaret

ANNA AND THE KING OF SIAM 2

⌛ 1860S 🌐 BANGKOK © 1944

Anna Harriette Crawford is offered a strange job. The King of Siam wants an educated English woman to teach his children the learning of the West. Anna does more than teach. Her stubbornness helps a reluctant king make many needed reforms. This is an amazing and sometimes hilarious biography.

Lanier, Sidney

THE BOY'S KING ARTHUR 2

⌛ MIDDLE AGES ⊕ ENGLAND © 1919

Sidney Lanier retells Sir Thomas Malory's stories of King Arthur.

Latham, Jean Lee

CARRY ON, MR. BOWDITCH 2

⌛ LATE 1700S – EARLY 1800S ⊕ MASSACHUSETTS & AROUND THE WORLD © 1955

Nathaniel Bowditch dreams of attending Harvard University but instead becomes an indentured servant to a ship's chandler. He studies advanced mathematics in the evenings and eventually gets a chance to go to sea. Nathaniel publishes *The American Practical Navigator,* which is still in use today.

THIS DEAR-BOUGHT LAND 1

⌛ EARLY 1600S ⊕ ENGLAND & AMERICA © 1957

In 1607 a young boy sails with settlers for Jamestown.

Lawrence, Iain

THE WRECKERS 2

⌛ EARLY 1800S ⊕ ENGLAND © 1998

Many ships wreck on the coast of Cornwall, England. The wreckers are a group of people who inhabit the coast and lure ships into the hazardous waters. When a ship wrecks, they salvage its cargo and sell it for profit. When John Spencer's ship is wrecked, he is the sole survivor. He learns of the wreckers' evil deeds and must escape from their clutches.

This book is well written with many characters and plot twists. It can be a bit gory at times, though.

THE SMUGGLERS 2

⌛ EARLY 1800S ⊕ ATLANTIC OCEAN © 1999

This book takes place a few months after *The Wreckers*. John's father buys the *Dragon*, which was once a smuggler ship. The Dragon's old captain rejoins the ship with some of his former crew, bringing trouble with him. Young John is again in a situation where he doesn't know whom to trust.

THE BUCCANEERS **2**

⏳ EARLY 1800S 🌐 ATLANTIC OCEAN © 2001

John and the *Dragon* sail from London for Jamaica. The crew finds a lifeboat on the sea with one sailor aboard. This book is third in the series.

Lawson, Robert

BEN AND ME **1**

⏳ 1700S 🌐 UNITED STATES & FRANCE © 1939

This is the life and adventures of Benjamin Franklin, as told by Amos, his mouse. Those familiar with people and events in Colonial America will enjoy this caricature. Robert Lawson's hilarious drawings make it even better.

RABBIT HILL **1**

⏳ MID-1900S 🌐 UNITED STATES © 1944

This is a story about rabbits, deer, squirrels, birds, and moles who live around an old country house. The animals notice with great excitement that new folks are moving into the house, which has stood empty for many years. The animals hope the new family will plant a garden, but they worry about dogs.

Lee, Harper

TO KILL A MOCKINGBIRD **3**

⏳ 1930S 🌐 ALABAMA © 1960

Jean Louise "Scout" Finch tells the story of growing up in sleepy Maycomb, Alabama. Often funny, often ordinary, always riveting, this story weaves adult issues into the world of a little girl. Jean's father is a lawyer and has been asked to defend a black man falsely accused of rape. The controversy forces his children to grow up quickly. Harper Lee addresses sensitive, sometimes unpleasant issues with humor and wisdom.

This may be my favorite book of all time. When Scout meets "Boo" Radley for the first time at the end of the book and puts her hand in his, I feel like crying.

Leighton, Margaret

JUDITH OF FRANCE 2

⏳ 800S 🌐 ENGLAND & FRANCE © 1948

Judith is Charlemagne's granddaughter. She is told she must marry the old king of England, but she loves someone else.

JOURNEY FOR A PRINCESS 2

⏳ 800S 🌐 ENGLAND & FRANCE © 1960

This is a sequel to *Judith of France*.

Lenski, Lois

STRAWBERRY GIRL 1

⏳ EARLY 1900S 🌐 FLORIDA © 1945

Birdie Boyer's family has moved into palmetto country with the idea of raising strawberries. When the Boyers begin cultivating their land, their neighbors the Slaters make trouble for them.

The unique setting of this story and its simple yet interesting plot make it a first-rate book for reading aloud.

SHOO-FLY GIRL 1

⏳ 1900S 🌐 PENNSYLVANIA © 1963

This is the story of Suzanna – Shoo-Fly – and her life as an Amish girl in Lancaster Country.

Lewis, C. S.

THE SCREWTAPE LETTERS 3

⏳ MID-1900S 🌐 ENGLAND © 1942

Screwtape is a devil, experienced in the arts of temptation, who is writing letters to his novice nephew Wormwood. These are funny and insightful perspectives from the "other side."

THE LION, THE WITCH AND THE WARDROBE 1

⏳ MID-1900S 🌐 ENGLAND & NARNIA © 1950

Peter, Susan, Edmund, and Lucy go into a wardrobe to hide from the housekeeper. Suddenly they find themselves in another world. They arrive just as Aslan, the lion, has returned to remove the curse of eternal winter placed on the land by the White Witch. But there is a traitor among them.

When I began reading this book, I thought that it would be boring, but after a few chapters, I could not put it down. *The Chronicles of Narnia* are some of my family's favorites to read aloud.

PRINCE CASPIAN 1

⌛ MID-1900S 🌐 ENGLAND & NARNIA © 1951

Narnia is again in trouble. A false king is on the throne, and Caspian, the true king, has called Peter, Susan, Edmund, and Lucy back into Narnia to help. In *Prince Caspian*, we meet the valiant mouse Reepicheep.

THE VOYAGE OF THE DAWN TREADER 1

⌛ MID-1900S 🌐 ENGLAND & NARNIA © 1952

A bracing, salty adventure begins as Edmund, Lucy, and Eustace Scrubb fall through a picture frame into the sea. King Caspian takes them on board for his journey to the ends of the world. The company faces serious dangers while discovering new islands. Selfish and obnoxious Eustace becomes a dragon in one memorable chapter.

THE SILVER CHAIR 1

⌛ MID-1900S 🌐 ENGLAND & NARNIA © 1953

Two children from our world and a Marshwiggle named Puddleglum must find the Underland to fulfill the mission Aslan gave them. They discover the importance of following Aslan's instructions and working together.

THE HORSE AND HIS BOY 1

⌛ FANTASY TIME 🌐 NARNIA © 1954

A boy, a girl, and two talking horses escape and journey towards Narnia. Aravis is a pampered aristocrat; Shasta is a slave. They share a common goal and find they need each other. A thrilling tale of narrow escapes, danger, chases, and surprises.

THE MAGICIAN'S NEPHEW 1

⌛ EARLY 1900S 🌐 ENGLAND & NARNIA © 1955

Crafty Uncle Andrew is experimenting, and before Polly and Digory know what has happened, they find themselves traveling between worlds. They witness the death of one world and the birth of Narnia. They accidentally bring a witch into London and then into Narnia. Rich in metaphors, this is one of the most unique stories in the Narnia chronicles.

THE LAST BATTLE 1

⌛ FANTASY TIME ⊕ NARNIA © 1956

Narnia has been infiltrated by evil. The ape Shift has convinced a weak donkey to pose as Aslan. All the talking creatures must choose sides. The good animals don't know who to believe. Friends from our world travel one last time to join Tirian, the last king, for Narnia's final battle.

LETTERS TO CHILDREN 1

⌛ MID-1900S ⊕ ENGLAND © 1985

This is a collection of letters and advice written by C. S. Lewis to children.

Lewis, Elizabeth Foreman

YOUNG FU OF THE UPPER YANGTZE 2

⌛ 1920S ⊕ CHINA © 1932

Young Fu and his mother Fu Be Be move from the country into the city of Chungking. Young Fu works as a coppersmith's apprentice. He must stay on his toes to navigate the dangers and opportunities the city brings him. This historical novel describes life in China during the turbulent 1920s.

WHEN THE TYPHOON BLOWS 1

⌛ 1930S ⊕ CHINA © 1942

A boy flees with his grandfather as the Japanese invade China.

Lindquist, Jennie

THE GOLDEN NAME DAY

⌛ EARLY 1900S ⊕ NEW ENGLAND © 1955

Nancy Bruce must live with her Swedish-American grandparents while her mother is in the hospital. She learns about Swedish customs, including the annual name days.

THE LITTLE SILVER HOUSE

⌛ EARLY 1900S ⊕ NEW ENGLAND © 1959

This is third in the series about Nancy Bruce.

THE CRYSTAL TREE

⌛ EARLY 1900S 🌐 NEW ENGLAND © 1966

This is a sequel to *The Golden Name Day.*

Lofting, Hugh

THE STORY OF DOCTOR DOLITTLE 1

⌛ 1800S 🌐 ENGLAND & AFRICA © 1920

Doctor Dolittle is called to Africa by the animals to heal the monkeys. Doctor Dolittle can understand almost every language in the world, including the languages of animals.

THE VOYAGES OF DOCTOR DOLITTLE 1

⌛ 1800S 🌐 ENGLAND & THE WORLD © 1922

Timmy Stubins has always wanted to be a naturalist, and when he meets Doctor Dolittle, he just might get his wish. Tommy and the Doctor go on a voyage of discovery and end up shipwrecked on the Floating Island.

London, Jack

THE CALL OF THE WILD 3

⌛ 1897 🌐 ALASKA © 1903

Buck is a large, intelligent black dog. He is stolen from his home in California and shipped to the Klondike in Alaska. Through abuse, he learns to hate humans. He becomes a respected lead dog for dog trains. Buck is befriended by Thornton, and with his legendary strength, he wins a thousand-dollar wager for Thornton. When his new master is killed by Indians – and with no remaining human ties – he answers "the call of the wild" and joins a wolf pack.

TALES OF THE FISH PATROL 2

⌛ LATE 1800S 🌐 SAN FRANCISCO BAY © 1905

Jack tells tales from his life as a law officer among the ruthless fishermen of San Francisco Bay.

WHITE FANG 3

⌛ LATE 1800S 🌐 YUKON © 1906

White Fang is half wolf and half dog born in the wild. He is raised in an Indian camp and is hated by the other dogs. This is the story of how White Fang gradually is civilized.

Lowry, Lois

NUMBER THE STARS **2**

⌛ 1943 🌐 DENMARK © 1989

This story is set in Denmark during the Nazi occupation. Ellen is Jewish and needs the help of Annemarie's family to survive.

MacDonald, George

THE GOLDEN KEY **2**

⌛ PAST 🌐 FAIRYLAND © 1867

Two children live on the border of fairyland. They search for the "land from where the shadows fall."

AT THE BACK OF THE NORTH WIND **2**

⌛ 1800S 🌐 ENGLAND & FANTASY © 1871

Diamond is a curious little boy who goes on dazzling adventures with his friend, the North Wind. This unusual book ties together several episodes of imagination and fantasy and invites readers to explore thoughts about God and life.

THE PRINCESS AND THE GOBLIN **2**

⌛ PAST 🌐 FANTASY © 1872

Curdie saves Princess Irene from the goblins, and she in turn saves Curdie.

THE LOST PRINCESS **2**

⌛ PAST 🌐 FANTASY © 1875

A wise woman must deal with two spoiled girls.

SIR GIBBIE **2**

⌛ MID-1800S 🌐 SCOTLAND © 1879

Gibbie is a ragged urchin who runs around an old Scottish city taking care of his father, a broken cobbler. When his father dies, Gibbie flees to the country. He meets many adventures and eventually comes into his father's lost inheritance.

My mother likes these sorts of stories.

THE PRINCESS AND CURDIE **2**

⌛ PAST 🌐 FANTASY © 1883

Curdie is sent to save Irene's father, accompanied by a strange creature called Lina. This is a sequel to *The Princess and the Goblin.*

MacLachlan, Patricia

SARAH, PLAIN AND TALL 1

⌛ LATE 1800S ⊕ MIDWEST AMERICA © 1985

Anna and Caleb live on a quiet, dusty farm. Their mother has died, and their father places a newspaper advertisement asking for a new wife. This brings Sarah from Maine. The new family learns about themselves and how to become a family.

Malot, Hector

THE ADVENTURES OF PERRINE 1

⌛ LATE 1800S ⊕ FRANCE © 1932

Perrine and her mother set out to find relatives who live in another town in France. When Perrine's mother dies, she must make her own living in an industrial town.

My mother loved this book when she read it a long time ago, though the plot was somewhat predictable.

THE ADVENTURES OF REMI 1

⌛ 1800S ⊕ FRANCE © 1878

Remi is an orphan who travels in search of someone to belong to.

Masefield, John

MARTIN HYDE 1

⌛ LATE 1600S ⊕ ENGLAND & HOLLAND © 1933

Young Martin Hyde becomes a messenger for the Duke of Monmouth, who is trying to capture the throne of England from James II. Martin has many adventures spying for the Duke and carrying secret messages.

McCloskey, Robert

HOMER PRICE 1

⌛ 1940S ⊕ UNITED STATES © 1943

Homer Price stops a robbery with his pet skunk, discovers that his superheroes are not what he thought they were, makes a few doughnuts, is captivated by a modern Pied Piper, and discovers that similitude is not a thing to be desired.

Younger children will love this story and its intriguing illustrations.

Meigs, Cornelia

THE TWO ARROWS 1

⌛ 1745 ⊕ ENGLAND © 1949

Jan and Ronald are arrested for disloyalty to King George II and deported to Maryland to serve seven years' indenture to Master James Hardwick.

WIND IN THE CHIMNEY 1

⌛ LATE 1700S ⊕ AMERICA © 1934

Widow Elizabeth Moreland arrives from England with three children. She is allowed to live near Valley Forge if she will make a quilt from a particular rare pattern.

Melville, Herman

MOBY-DICK 3

⌛ EARLY 1800S ⊕ OCEAN © 1851

"Call me Ishmael." Ishmael signs aboard the whaling ship Pequod with Captain Ahab. Ahab does not hunt for whales, but for one whale – the white whale.

Miller, Olive Beaupre

MY BOOK HOUSE 1

⌛ ANCIENT & MODERN TIME ⊕ WORLD © 1920

Each volume of this series is designed for a different grade level. Selections come from writers like Swift, Stevenson, and Kipling.

Milne, A. A.

WHEN WE WERE VERY YOUNG 1

⌛ EARLY 1900S ⊕ ENGLAND © 1924

This is a collection of humorous poems for children.

WINNIE-THE-POOH 1

⌛ FANTASY TIME ⊕ ENGLAND © 1926

These humorous tales of Christopher Robin's stuffed animals in their make-believe world are good for reading aloud to children. They are entertaining for adults because of the subtle jokes and commentary on the way people think and behave.

NOW WE ARE SIX 1

⏳ EARLY 1900S 🌐 ENGLAND © 1927

These light-hearted and clever poems about childhood's fantasies center around Christopher Robin, famous for being the owner of Winnie-the-Pooh.

THE HOUSE AT POOH CORNER 1

⏳ FANTASY TIME 🌐 ENGLAND © 1928

This is the second book of stories about Winnie-the-Pooh. Here we are introduced to Tigger, and at the end, learn that Christopher Robin is going to leave. Chapters include "In Which a House Is Built at Pooh Corner for Eeyore," "In Which Tigger Comes to the Forest and Has Breakfast," and "In Which a Search Is Organized and Piglet Nearly Meets the Heffalump Again."

Montgomery, L. M.

ANNE OF GREEN GABLES 2

⏳ EARLY 1900S 🌐 PRINCE EDWARD ISLAND © 1908

Anne Shirley is an orphan girl accidentally adopted – instead of a boy – by Marilla and Matthew Cuthbert. The tempestuous, mischievous, imaginative world of Anne Shirley meets the quiet, conservative world of Avonlea. This book has wonderful, memorable characters and adventures.

ANNE OF AVONLEA 2

⏳ EARLY 1900S 🌐 PRINCE EDWARD ISLAND © 1909

Anne is now a teacher in Avonlea. She helps Marilla run the farm and care for two orphans at Green Gables. Though she is growing up, Anne retains her sense of humor and propensity for mischief.

For reasons I do not understand, my sisters eat up this very long series of books.

PAT OF SILVER BUSH 2

⏳ EARLY 1900S 🌐 PRINCE EDWARD ISLAND © 1933

Patricia Gardiner hates changes in her world. She loves her family's farm, Silver Bush, more than anything. Judy Plum is the loving, funny housekeeper employed by Pat's family and one of the book's most memorable characters.

MISTRESS PAT 2

⏳ EARLY 1900S 🌐 PRINCE EDWARD ISLAND © 1935

Pat is content to stay at home and enjoy the life she has loved since she was a little girl. But everything around her is changing. Pat must accept growing up and let go of the past.

Moody, Ralph

LITTLE BRITCHES 1

⏳ 1906-1910 🌐 COLORADO © 1950

"Father and I were ranchers." Ralph Moody tells how his father moved their family to a ranch at the foot of the Rockies. They try to scratch out a living in that beautiful, dry land.

Morey, Walt

GENTLE BEN 1

⏳ MID-1900S 🌐 ALASKA © 1965

Mark Andersen adopts a brown bear. This story follows the adventures and consequences of raising a bear.

KAVIK, THE WOLF DOG 1

⏳ 1900S 🌐 ALASKA © 1968

Andy Evans rescues Kavik from a plane crash and wins the dog's affection. When Andy enters Kavik in the North American Sled Dog Derby, Kavik's legal owner shows up and claims the dog. Kavik runs away and travels two hundred miles back to Andy.

Morrison, Lucile

THE LOST QUEEN OF EGYPT 2

⏳ ANCIENT TIME 🌐 EGYPT © 1937

The story of Ankhsenpaaten, King Tutankhamon's wife.

Mukerji, Dhan Gopal

GAY-NECK 1

⏳ WORLD WAR ONE 🌐 INDIA © 1927

Gay-Neck is a carrier pigeon who is raised by a lad to carry messages through the air. The lad gives the bird to serve in World War One, where Gay-Neck experiences many dangers.

Mulock, Dinah Maria

THE LITTLE LAME PRINCE 1

⧗ PAST ⊕ FANTASY © 1875

Prince Dolor is injured in a careless accident when he is a baby. When his mother and father both die, the prince's uncle takes his throne and sends Dolor to live in a lonely tower far away. Dolor's fairy godmother allows him to experience the outside world.

This book illustrates the moral, "We cannot have things as we want them to be, . . . we must learn to bear them and make the best of them."

Nesbit, Edith

THE STORY OF THE TREASURE SEEKERS 2

⧗ LATE 1800S ⊕ ENGLAND © 1898

When the Bastable family loses its fortune, the children take it upon themselves to restore it. They try various profit-making ideas, including publishing a newspaper and kidnapping.

FIVE CHILDREN AND IT 1

⧗ EARLY 1900S ⊕ ENGLAND © 1902

Robert, Anthea, Jane, Cyril, and the Baby discover a Sand Fairy who grants wishes. This discovery is more complicated than it appears. The Sand Fairy is stubborn and unmanageable, and no matter how good the children's wishes seem when they make them, the children end up in serious trouble.

Nesbit's fast-moving tale of mishaps will keep readers laughing.

THE RAILWAY CHILDREN 1

⧗ EARLY 1900S ⊕ ENGLAND © 1906

When their father mysteriously leaves, Roberta, Peter, and Phyllis move with their mother to a country house near a railway station. The siblings relish their new life among the trains. They make new friends, help people in trouble, and solve mysteries.

The adventures of the Railway Children are a family favorite.

North, Sterling

CAPTURED BY THE MOHAWKS 1

⌛ 1600S ⊕ NORTHERN AMERICA © 1960

At age sixteen, Pierre is captured and adopted by the Mohawks.

RASCAL 1

⌛ 1918 ⊕ MIDWEST AMERICA © 1963

Rascal is a very funny raccoon owned by Sterling North when he was eleven years old. The two become inseparably attached to one another for one year.

My sister has adopted four raccoons, proving this book is completely true.

Norton, Mary

THE BORROWERS 1

⌛ 1900 ⊕ ENGLAND © 1952

Arrietty Clock is six inches tall and belongs to a race of people who "borrow" things from the big people. Arrietty and her parents, Hoily and Pod, live in a hole under the floor. One day Arrietty makes friends with a dreaded Human Bean. When her family is in danger, the Human Bean helps Arrietty's family escape from a ferret, set upon them by the housekeeper Mrs. Driver.

One of my favorite books when I was young. This story introduces us to the world from the perspective of people six inches tall.

THE BORROWERS AFIELD 1

⌛ 1900 ⊕ ENGLAND © 1955

The Clock family settles into a boot embedded in the bank of a stream.

THE BORROWERS AFLOAT 1

⌛ 1900 ⊕ ENGLAND © 1959

The Clock family escape to Spiller's streamside teakettle home.

THE BORROWERS ALOFT 1

⌛ 1900 ⊕ ENGLAND © 1961

The Clock family takes a ride in a balloon.

THE BORROWERS AVENGED 1

⌛ 1900 ⊕ ENGLAND © 1982

The Clock family escapes from the attic and sets up house in an old rectory.

O'Dell, Scott

ISLAND OF THE BLUE DOLPHINS 1

⌛ EARLY 1800S ⊕ SAN NICHOLAS ISLAND © 1960

Karana and her tribe live on a island off the coast of California. When missionaries come to take them to the mainland, Karana and her brother Ramo are accidentally left behind. When Ramo is killed by wild dogs, Karana must scratch out a living alone on the small island. This story of survival and simple adventure is one of my mother's favorites.

THE KING'S FIFTH 1

⌛ EARLY 1500S ⊕ SPANISH AMERICA © 1966

Esteban de Sandoval works as a map maker in the New World. He joins an expedition to discover the golden cities of Cibola. Esteban cares nothing for the gold but only for the maps he will make. The expedition finds a native city where a religious rite has coated the bottom of the lake with gold dust. The expedition leaders trick the Indians, drain the lake, and take the gold dust. Empty-handed, Esteban is the only member to return alive. The Inquisitors put him to trial for murder and for withholding the king's tax of one fifth of the treasure. This story teaches what greedy people will do for gold.

THE BLACK PEARL 1

⌛ PAST ⊕ BAJA CALIFORNIA © 1967

Ramón wants to be a man and dive for pearls. His teacher tells him never to dive into the hidden cave where a giant manta lives. He does not listen and dives to find a rare black pearl in the cave, but the pearl only brings misfortune.

THE HAWK THAT DARE NOT HUNT BY DAY 2

⌛ KING HENRY VIII ⊕ ENGLAND © 1975

This is the story of Tyndale's English translation of the Bible and how the printed volumes were smuggled into England.

O'Hara, Mary

MY FRIEND FLICKA 3

⌛ EARLY 1900S 🌐 WYOMING © 1941

Ken McLaughlin lives on a ranch in Wyoming with his filly Flicka, who has questionable bloodlines. Ken must surmount his father's disapproval of Flicka as Ken and the horse grow together.

Ollivant, Alfred

BOB, SON OF BATTLE 3

⌛ LATE 1800S 🌐 SCOTLAND © 1898

Hoo aboot sich a yarn that'll bring the tares to the eyes o' e'en the sternest mon. This book is about Bob, a bonnie tyke and last of the Gray Dogs of Kenmuir; Davie, a puir mitherless lad; and his fether, Adam M'Adam, a little man turned harsh after the death of his wife.

My mother says this is the saddest book she ever read.

Orczy, Baroness

THE SCARLET PIMPERNEL 2

⌛ 1793-94 🌐 ENGLAND & FRANCE © 1905

The Scarlet Pimpernel is the talk of London. He is the mysterious hero who continues to save French aristocrats from the terrible embrace of Madame la Guillotine. But Lady Blakeny has been blackmailed by the French ambassador to help him unmask the Scarlet Pimpernel. She discovers too late who the Pimpernel really is.

One of our family's favorite books to read aloud. This story is a mystery, an adventure, and a romance.

THE ELUSIVE PIMPERNEL 2

⌛ LATE 1700S 🌐 ENGLAND & FRANCE © 1908

Chauvelin is determined to get revenge on the Scarlet Pimpernel. This is a sequel to *The Scarlet Pimpernel.*

ELDORADO 2

⌛ LATE 1700S 🌐 ENGLAND & FRANCE © 1913

The Scarlet Pimpernel tries to rescue the young Dauphin. This is a sequel to *The Scarlet Pimpernel.*

THE LEAGUE OF THE SCARLET PIMPERNEL — 2

⌛ LATE 1700S ⊕ ENGLAND & FRANCE © 1919

This is a collection of Scarlet Pimpernel stories.

Orwell, George

ANIMAL FARM — 3

⌛ EARLY 1900S ⊕ A FARM © 1946

The animals are tired of working for the farmer. This is the story of their great revolution. They drive the farmer off the farm and declare themselves free and everyone equal – though some are more equal than others.

This is a classic satire on Marxism.

Otis, James

TOBY TYLER, OR TEN WEEKS WITH A CIRCUS — 1

⌛ 1800S ⊕ AMERICA © 1881

Toby runs away from his uncle's farm to join the circus. He learns the circus isn't what he thought it was.

Page, Thomas Nelson

IN OLE VIRGINIA — 3

⌛ MID-1800S ⊕ VIRGINIA © 1887

This is collection of short stories around the Civil War, told in an old Southern dialect.

TWO LITTLE CONFEDERATES — 2

⌛ 1860S ⊕ VIRGINIA © 1888

"Two Little Patriots" and "Among the Camps" are short stories centered around the South during the Civil War. These are cute stories, some of which will make you cry.

RED ROCK: A CHRONICLE OF RECONSTRUCTION — 3

⌛ MID-1800S ⊕ SOUTHEASTERN AMERICA © 1898

This is a story of life in the south after the Civil War, when the carpetbaggers were in power. A Southern man loves a Northern girl, and a Northern man loves a Southern girl.

Paine, Lauran

THE OPEN RANGE MEN 3

⌛ 1880S ⊕ WESTERN AMERICA © 1990

Boss Spearman and his men feed cattle on the open range. When a local rancher tries to take their herd, Boss's men fight to save their lives.

Lauran Paine has a clear and descriptive writing style. He helps us understand his characters by describing what they do.

Parkman, Francis

THE OREGON TRAIL 3

⌛ EARLY 1800S ⊕ WESTERN AMERICA © 1849

This is the story of Parkman's 1700-mile journey around Nebraska, Wyoming, Colorado, and Kansas. Much of the book covers three weeks when Parkman hunted buffalo with the Oglala Sioux.

Pease, Howard

LONG WHARF 1

⌛ 1850S ⊕ SAN FRANCISCO © 1939

Danny Mason and his father are left on their ship in the San Francisco harbor when their crew deserts for the California gold fields. When Captain Mason also catches the gold germ, Danny is left to watch the ship. Danny waits and waits. With the help of friends on shore, Danny turns his ship into a shop and boarding house.

SHIPWRECK 1

⌛ 1800S ⊕ SEA © 1957

Renny Mitchum is mess boy aboard the trading schooner *Samarang*.

Porter, Eleanor H.

POLLYANNA 1

⌛ EARLY 1900S ⊕ UNITED STATES © 1913

Pollyanna is an orphan living with her severe aunt. Her sunshine invades her aunt's world and transforms the lives of the community. Pollyanna is the world's most famous optimist. She is ridiculed for her stubbornly hopeful outlook. We could all use a bit more of her attitude.

POLLYANNA GROWS UP 1

⏳ EARLY 1900S 🌐 BOSTON © 1915

Pollyanna returns to Boston, where she wins hearts just as she did with Aunt Polly. This is a sequel to *Pollyanna*.

Porter, Jane

THADEUS OF WARSAW 3

⏳ LATE 1700S 🌐 POLAND & ENGLAND © 1803

Thadeus Sobieski fights to free Poland from Russia. He loses his lands and the Russians burn the Sobieski palace. He travels to England where he meets more adventures.

THE SCOTTISH CHIEFS 3

⏳ LATE 1200S 🌐 SCOTLAND © 1809

The story of William Wallace's fight against the English King Edward.

Potter, Beatrix

CHILDREN'S PICTURE BOOKS 1

⏳ 1800S 🌐 ENGLAND © 1902-1930

Beatrix Potter wrote twenty-four little books for young children, but the expansive vocabulary, clever story-telling, humor, and Beatrix Potter's own watercolors appeal to all ages. These small white-jacketed volumes, designed to fit small hands, contain some of the world's most famous animal characters and teach many good lessons in character.

Potter's stories include: *The Tale of Peter Rabbit* (1902), *The Tale of Squirrel Nutkin* (1903), *The Tailor of Gloucester* (1903), *The Tale of Benjamin Bunny* (1904), *The Tale of Two Bad Mice* (1904), *The Tale of Mrs. Tiggy-Winkle* (1905), *The Tale of the Pie and the Patty Pan* (1905), *The Tale of Mr. Jeremy Fisher* (1906), *The Story of a Fierce Bad Rabbit* (1906), *The Story of Miss Moppet* (1906), *The Tale of Tom Kitten* (1907), *The Tale of Jemima Puddle-Duck* (1908), *The Tale of Samuel Whiskers or The Roly-Poly Pudding* (1908), *The Tale of the Flopsy Bunnies* (1909), *The Tale of Ginger and Pickles* (1909), *The Tale of Mrs. Tittlemouse* (1910), *The Tale of Timmy Tiptoes* (1911), *The Tale of Mr. Tod* (1912), *The Tale of Pigling Bland* (1913), *Appley Dapply's Nursery Rhymes* (1917), *The*

Tale of Johnny Town-Mouse (1918), *Cecily Parsley's Nursery Rhymes* (1922), *The Fairy Caravan* (1929), and *The Tale of Little Pig Robinson* (1930).

Prentiss, Elizabeth

STEPPING HEAVENWARD 3

⌛ 1800S ⊕ UNITED STATES © 1869

This is the fictional journal of Katherine, begun in 1815 when she is sixteen years old. Katherine writes frankly about her troubles and striving, as she humanly seeks to be closer to God.

Pyle, Howard

THE MERRY ADVENTURES OF ROBIN HOOD 2

⌛ MIDDLE AGES ⊕ ENGLAND © 1883

Many Robin Hood legends and ballads are retold here with the usual characters: Little John, Will Scarlet, Allan a Dale, and Friar Tuck.

WITHIN THE CAPES 2

⌛ 1812 ⊕ NEW ENGLAND & ATLANTIC © 1885

This is the story of a Quaker, Tom Granger, and how he tries to win permission to marry a young woman by showing himself responsible. He is shipwrecked on a desert island and thinks all his hopes have ended, until he discovers something in the sand.

OTTO OF THE SILVER HAND 2

⌛ MIDDLE AGES ⊕ GERMANY © 1888

Little Otto is a motherless child born amidst the wars of the German robber-barons. His father, Baron Conrad, is one of those cruel lords. While Baron Conrad is called away to the royal court of the new Emperor Baron, Henry of Trutz-Drachen comes by night, takes Castle Drachenhausen, and with the boy Otto captive, returns to his own castle. When Baron Conrad comes home, he finds few remaining men-at-arms still loyal to him. He goes to Baron Henry's castle and tries to free his son. Otto's misfortunes, though no fault of his own, and the loyalty of his father's men-at-arms in risking their lives to save him, will stretch your heart's ligaments.

Good for reading aloud, this is one of our family's most favorite.

MEN OF IRON 2

⏳ 1400-1412 🌐 ENGLAND © 1891

Myles Falworth was eight when his blind father and family fled to holy sanctuary to escape the anger of King Henry IV. When Myles is sixteen, his father sends him to serve the Earl of Mackworth as a page and learn the skills of chivalry. Myles meets with many boyhood adventures and gains the respect of the Earl. The dark knight who was the cause of the Falworth misfortunes is the Earl of Alban. Myles swears to avenge his father's blindness and dishonor and throws down the gauntlet in the presence of the king.

When mother came to the end of this book, my sisters were crying and we boys had decided what to be when we grew up.

THE ROSE OF PARADISE 2

⏳ 1720 🌐 AFRICA COAST © 1894

"This being a detailed account of certain adventures that happened to Captain John Mackra, in connection with the famous pirate, Edward England, in the year 1720, off the island of Juanna in the Mozambique Channel; writ by himself, and now for the first time published."

THE STORY OF KING ARTHUR AND HIS KNIGHTS 2

⌛ MIDDLE AGES ⊕ ENGLAND © 1903

Young Arthur gets everyone's attention when he draws the sword from the stone. Pyle said "King Arthur was the most honorable, gentle Knight who ever lived in all the world" and was a "perfect example of courage and humility that anyone might do exceedingly well to follow after their manner of behavior in such measure as he is able to do."

THE STORY OF THE CHAMPIONS OF THE ROUND TABLE 2

⌛ MIDDLE AGES ⊕ ENGLAND © 1905

Here are the adventures of Sir Lancelot, Sir Tristam, and Sir Percival.

THE STORY OF SIR LANCELOT AND HIS COMPANIONS 2

⌛ MIDDLE AGES ⊕ ENGLAND © 1907

We read of Lancelot's daring rescue of Queen Guinevere, the tournament at Astolat, and the birth of Galahad.

THE STORY OF THE GRAIL AND THE PASSING OF ARTHUR 2

⌛ MIDDLE AGES ⊕ ENGLAND © 1910

This book recounts the adventures of Sir Galahad, "the most perfect knight who ever lived," and the final days of King Arthur.

THE WONDER CLOCK 2

⌛ PAST ⊕ THE WORLD © 1912

Here are twenty-four stories, one for each hour of the day. These are full of heroes, bravery, and wits.

Rankin, Carroll Watson

DANDELION COTTAGE 1

⌛ EARLY 1900S ⊕ MICHIGAN © 1904

The story of four girls' summer adventures in a little house of their own. Jean, Bettie, Marjory, and Mabel earn the rent for an old, unused house by digging up the dandelions and weeds in the yard. They keep house the whole summer and meet many nice people and a few not-so-nice ones. An amusing book for young girls.

THE ADOPTING OF ROSA MARIE 1

⌛ EARLY 1900S ⊕ MICHIGAN © 1908

This sequel to *Dandelion Cottage* tells of the four girls' play at being little mothers. Mabel finds a baby to take care of, but the baby's real mother disappears, causing the girls new adventures.

CINDER POND 1

⌛ 1900S ⊕ NORTHERN AMERICA © 1915

Jeannette Huntington Duval and her family are squatters who live in shanties built on a crumbling dock jutting into Lake Superior.

GYPSY NAN 1

⌛ EARLY 1900S ⊕ MICHIGAN © 1926

After little Nancy Linden loses her mother, her father must go to South America, leaving Nancy with her Aunt Ellen. Nancy's aunt thinks she is a wild child.

WOLF ROCK 1

⌛ 1900S ⊕ NORTHERN AMERICA © 1933

This is a sequel to *Cinder Pond.*

Rankin, Louise

DAUGHTER OF THE MOUNTAINS 1

⌛ 1800S ⊕ TIBET, NEPAL & INDIA © 1948

Momo wants a Lhasa puppy, but this is too expensive for her family. When she is given a Lhasa, she names it Pempa. Pempa is stolen, and Momo must travel through Tibet, Nepal, Bhutan, and India to retrieve her dog.

Ransome, Arthur

SWALLOWS AND AMAZONS 2

⌛ EARLY 1900S ⊕ ENGLAND © 1930

John, Susan, Titty, and Roger are given the use of a small boat, the *Swallow*. They have a wonderfully free time on their lake and find an island for their own. But they discover they are not the only children on the lake. They go to war with the Amazons, Nancy and Peggy Blackett, but later become friends.

This is the story of childhood freedom and play, and it remains one of my favorites.

Rawicz, Slavomir

THE LONG WALK 3

⌛ WORLD WAR TWO 🌐 RUSSIA, SIBERIA, MONGOLIA, TIBET & INDIA © 1955

This is the grueling story of Slavomir Rawicz, a Polish cavalry man taken prisoner by the Russians at the beginning of World War Two. After enduring nearly a year of torture, he is sent to a prison in Siberia. But Slavomir is a survivor. With several other inmates, he escapes and walks four thousand miles from Siberia, across the Gobi Desert and the Himalaya mountains into India.

Rawlings, Marjorie Kinnan

THE YEARLING 2

⌛ LATE 1800S 🌐 FLORIDA © 1938

The Yearling is an orphaned fawn. The fawn's mother was killed for her liver, which was used to draw out poison from Mr. Baxter's snake bite. Jody Baxter raises the little deer and names it Flag. He loves his pet, even when it eats the young corn shoots that Jody plants, but his mother fears they may starve without the corn.

This book is one of my mother's favorites to read aloud. This story concerns a young boy as he matures to adolescence.

Rawls, Wilson

WHERE THE RED FERN GROWS 2

⌛ 1930-40S 🌐 OZARK MOUNTAINS © 1961

Billy Colman spends all his free time for two years saving up money to buy two redbone coonhounds. He names them Little Ann and Old Dan and trains them to hunt 'coons. Through their adventures in the Ozarks, the trio become inseparable. Billy's hounds compete in the regional raccoon hunt.

The ending to this tale of true devotion between a boy and his dogs is famous for its ability to bring tears to readers' eyes. This book is one of my mother's favorites.

Rounds, Glen

THE BLIND COLT 1

⏳ MID-1900S 🌐 WESTERN AMERICA © 1941

A little blue-gray colt is born blind but succeeds in living with the wild herd despite its handicap. When Whitey sees the colt, he sets himself to catch and tame it. The two become fast friends.

I loved this story and its unique illustrations when I was young.

WHITEY AND THE COLT KILLER 1

⏳ EARLY 1900S 🌐 WESTERN AMERICA © 1962

Whitey and his pinto colt fight a prairie fire and a wolf that has been killing calves.

BLIND OUTLAW 1

⏳ EARLY 1900S 🌐 WESTERN AMERICA © 1980

A boy who cannot speak tames a blind horse.

Russell, W. Clark

THE WRECK OF THE GROSVENOR 2

⏳ 1800S 🌐 ATLANTIC © 1877

Mr. Royle is the new second mate of the *Grosvenor.* When the ship's stores are found to be inedible, the captain refuses to take on new stores. When the captain refuses to save shipwrecked survivors, Mr. Royle forcefully saves Mary Robertson and her father, for which the captain puts him in irons. The crew mutinies, kills the captain, and forces Mr. Royle to steer them to America.

This book is one of our family's favorites. This story gives a picture of the inhumane treatment of sailors at that time.

JOHN HOLDSWORTH, CHIEF MATE 2

⌛ 1800S 🌐 ATLANTIC © 1884

John Holdsworth leaves his new wife in England and sails as mate of a ship bound for America. The ship is wrecked, and in the trauma of exposure on the open sea, John loses his memory.

Ruthin, Margaret

ELLI OF THE NORTHLAND 1

⌛ MID-1900S 🌐 LAPLAND & FINLAND © 1961

Elli Sara lives in Lapland with her grandparents and brother. She always thought her parents were killed in the war between the Russians and the Germans. But now her brother tells her two men have come to take her to her father, who is a rich man of Finland.

Rutgers van der Loeff, A.

AVALANCHE! 1

⌛ MID-1900S 🌐 SWISS ALPS © 1957

Werner is caught in an avalanche that buries his village. He cannot find his parents and aids in the rescue work.

Sachar, Louis

HOLES 2

⌛ LATE 1900S 🌐 TEXAS © 1998

Stanley Yelnats IV is sent to a boy's juvenile detention center for stealing a pair of sneakers. At Camp Green Lake, the boys dig holes all day – to build character. It takes Stanley a while to figure out what they're really digging for.

St. John, Patricia

TREASURES OF THE SNOW 1

⌛ 1900S 🌐 SWITZERLAND © 1950

Annette cares for her little brother Dani after their mother dies. Through the carelessness of Lucien, Dani is injured. Annette is filled with hatred and determines to have revenge. Lucien wants to atone for his mistake, but Annette refuses to forgive him. This story of the Swiss Alps teaches lessons in repentance and forgiveness.

TWICE FREED 2

⌛ MID-AD 100S 🌐 PALESTINE © 1987

This story tells how Onesimus was freed from slavery.

STAR OF LIGHT 1

⌛ 1900S 🌐 NORTH AFRICA © 1995

Hamid and his blind sister Kinza escape from their stepfather. They make their way to Morocco, where they are found by an English missionary nurse.

THREE GO SEARCHING 2

⌛ 1900S 🌐 AFRICA © 1995

David's father is a missionary doctor in Africa, where their family lives. David and Waffi befriend a destitute servant girl, Lela. The three experience adventure as they learn what it means to follow Christ.

Salten, Felix

BAMBI: A LIFE IN THE WOODS 1

⌛ TIME OF GUNS 🌐 EUROPEAN WOODS © 1923

Bambi is a roe fawn born in the deep glades and meadows of old-growth forest. He and his cousins Faline and Bobo experience a happy-go-lucky fawnhood. Their life changes when a dreaded new creature comes with the arm that throws death. Bambi's mother is killed by a hunting party, and Bambi must fend for himself.

A story of simple nature and maturing character, this book is good for reading aloud.

Scott, Sir Walter

WAVERLY 3

⏳ 1745 🌐 ENGLAND & SCOTLAND © 1814

Edward Waverley is sent to Scotland during the Jacobite Rebellion. He travels north into the Highlands and the heart of the uprising.

ROB ROY 3

⏳ EARLY 1700S 🌐 ENGLAND & SCOTLAND © 1817

Frank Osbaldistone quarrels with his father and is sent to live with his uncle. During a Jacobite Rising, Frank goes to the Scottish Highlands to collect a debt. There he meets Rob Roy MacGregor.

IVANHOE 3

⏳ 1194 🌐 ENGLAND © 1820

Wilfred of Ivanhoe has returned from the Crusades and is still in love with the beautiful Rowena. This story has such a complex plot it is impossible to describe in one short review. The story is set in the time when cruel King John acted as regent of England, during his brother Richard's absence. We learn what it means for a chivalrous knight to sacrifice his life to save a beautiful damsel from a terrible fate.

KENILWORTH 3

⏳ 1500S 🌐 ENGLAND © 1821

Robert Dudley, Earl of Leicester, secretly marries Amy Robsart. Amy loves her husband, and he loves her, but his ambition gets in his way. In the end, he surrenders his pride and confesses his marriage to Queen Elizabeth.

PEVERIL OF THE PEAK 3

⏳ LATE 1600S 🌐 ENGLAND © 1823

Sir Geoffrey Peveril is a Cavalier, while his friend Major Bridgenorth is a staunch Puritan. The strife between the Cavaliers and the Roundheads (Puritans) during the reign of Charles II drives these two friends apart. This is the love story of their children, Julian Peveril and Alice Bridgenorth, intertwined with the intrigues of Charles II's court and the dangers of the 'Popish Plot.'

QUENTIN DURWARD 3

⌛ 1400S ⊕ FRANCE © 1823

Quentin leaves Scotland to become a mercenary for Louis XI of France.

THE TALISMAN 3

⌛ 1100S ⊕ PALESTINE © 1825

Sir Kenneth follows King Richard the Lion-Hearted to the Holy Land in the Third Crusade. Kenneth loves the Lady Edith Plantagenet, Richard's kinswoman. King Richard is ill with fever and unable to fight the Moslems. The other leaders seek peace with Saladin, leader of the Moslems, but for their own advantage. Sir Kenneth brings a Moslem physician with a mysterious talisman to heal the king. The plot deepens as the other leaders try to break up the crusade.

This story is one of Scott's best novels, with many surprises and twists of fortune.

Seredy, Kate

THE GOOD MASTER 1

⌛ EARLY 1900S ⊕ HUNGARY © 1935

Jancsi is the son of a well-respected Hungarian farmer, called the Good Master. Kate, Jancsi's cousin, has come to live with Jancsi's family. Kate tries to keep up with her cousin and soon learns to manage animals as well as he does. The two become best friends and share adventures on the farm, including a tangle with gypsies and a horse roundup.

This story is rich with details about life and traditions in old Hungary.

THE WHITE STAG 1

⌛ 400S ⊕ ASIA & EUROPE © 1937

Attila the Hun is the father of the Hungarian nation. This is the story of how the Huns migrated from Asia to Central Europe in AD 400.

Serraillier, Ian

THE SILVER SWORD 1

⌛ 1940S ⊕ WARSAW © 1959

Three children try to find their parents after their mother is captured by the Germans.

Sewell, Anna

BLACK BEAUTY **2**

⏳ 1800S 🌐 ENGLAND © 1877

In this autobiography, a horse named Black Beauty relates how the first few years of his life were equine bliss. But he soon learns animals are at the mercy of their masters. He is sold to many owners with varying degrees of humanity or inhumanity.

This story shows us how a horse might see the world.

Seyfert, Ella Maie

LITTLE AMISH SCHOOLHOUSE **1**

⏳ 1800S 🌐 PENNSYLVANIA © 1939

Martha and David Wegner live in an Amish community in Pennsylvania.

Sharp, Margery

THE RESCUERS **2**

⏳ 1900S 🌐 NEW YORK & EUROPE © 1959

An organization of mice called "The Prisoners' Aid Society" learns of a Norwegian poet imprisoned in the Black Castle. Bernard, Bianca, and Nils set off to rescue him.

A wonderful story with lots of humor, this book is hard to put down.

Sheldon, Charles M.

IN HIS STEPS **3**

⏳ LATE 1800S 🌐 UNITED STATES © 1897

Henry Maxwell is working on his Sunday sermon when he is visited by a tramp. The tramp challenges the minster and his congregation to change their definition of discipleship. A band of Christians decides to ask, "What would Jesus do?"

Shemin, Margaretha

THE LITTLE RIDERS **1**

⏳ WORLD WAR TWO 🌐 HOLLAND © 1963

Johanna lives with her grandparents in Nazi-occupied Holland. Johanna and her grandfather care for the "little riders," which are part of the town's church clock mechanism. Johanna and her grandparents learn the Germans want to confiscate the little riders for scrap metal, and they work to save them.

Sidney, Margaret

FIVE LITTLE PEPPERS AND HOW THEY GREW 1

⧗ 1800S ⊕ AMERICA © 1881

This series of books tells the story of the Pepper family after Mr. Pepper dies. They deal with poverty and the looming fear of starvation. Five children – Ben, Polly, Davie, Joel, and Phronsie – help their "Mamsie" make a meager living. Mamsie can't ever seem to stop being the "goodest" there is.

Smith, Dodie

THE HUNDRED AND ONE DALMATIANS 1

⧗ EARLY 1900S ⊕ ENGLAND © 1956

Pongo and Missis Pongo are Dalmatians who live with their pets, Mr. and Mrs. Dearly. When Cruella de Vil steals Pongo and Missis' puppies to make a fur coat, the two parent dogs use the network of "Twilight Barking" to start a rescue.

Snedeker, Caroline Dale

THERAS AND HIS TOWN 1

⧗ ANCIENT TIME ⊕ GREECE © 1924

Theras was born in Athens but is taken to Sparta when his father dies in war. There he is trained in the harsh Spartan education system. He escapes and heads for Athens.

This book explains the important differences between Athens and Sparta.

DOWNRIGHT DENCY 1

⧗ EARLY 1800S ⊕ NANTUCKET ISLAND © 1927

Dencey gets mad at Jetsam and throws a stone at him. As punishment he asks her to teach him to read.

LUKE'S QUEST 1

⧗ ANCIENT TIME ⊕ MEDITERRANEAN © 1947

A fictionalized biography of the apostle Luke.

Snicket, Lemony (Daniel Handler)

A SERIES OF UNFORTUNATE EVENTS

Violet, Klaus, and Sunny Baudelaire's parents are killed in a fire at the family mansion. They are adopted by various bad or foolish people, and everywhere they turn, they discover Count Olaf is trying to steal their family fortune. Lemony Snicket – who has done extensive research on the Baudelaires – warns us this story is a miserable one and suggests we stop reading immediately.

THE BAD BEGINNING **2**

⌛ MID-1900S 🌐 THE WORLD © 1999

Soon after the Baudelaire children are orphaned, they are taken to their new guardian, Count Olaf, a distant relative. He puts their sister Sunny in a cage and refuses to release her until Violet promises to marry him.

THE REPTILE ROOM **2**

⌛ MID-1900S 🌐 THE WORLD © 1999

The Baudelaire children are adopted by their uncle Monty, a herpetologist. Trouble with Count Olaf ensues, involving an incredibly deadly viper.

THE WIDE WINDOW **2**

⌛ MID-1900S 🌐 THE WORLD © 2000

After the death of their uncle Monty, the Baudelaire children are adopted by their Aunt Josephine, who is frightened of nearly everything.

THE MISERABLE MILL **2**

⌛ MID-1900S 🌐 THE WORLD © 2000

The Baudelaire children come to work at the Lucky Smells Lumber Mill. They are subjected to multiple child labor violations.

THE AUSTERE ACADEMY **2**

⌛ MID-1900S 🌐 THE WORLD © 2000

The Baudelaire children receive an education at Prufrock Preparatory School. They learn the mysterious initials V.F.D. have a special meaning.

THE ERSATZ ELEVATOR **2**

⌛ MID-1900S 🌐 THE WORLD © 2001

The Baudelaire children are sent to live at the top of a tall building with Esme and Jerome Squalor. They quickly discover they need to climb down the elevator shaft to safety.

THE VILE VILLAGE **2**

⌛ MID-1900S 🌐 THE WORLD © 2001

The Baudelaire children's final guardian is an entire village – the Village of Foul Devotees. Here the children are accused of committing murder.

THE HOSTILE HOSPITAL **2**

⌛ MID-1900S 🌐 THE WORLD © 2001

After being falsely accused of murder, the Baudelaire children take refuge in the ruined half of Heimlich Hospital. Here Count Olaf's henchmen attempt to perform a very unnecessary operation on Violet.

THE CARNIVOROUS CARNIVAL **2**

⌛ MID-1900S 🌐 THE WORLD © 2002

The Baudelaire children escape in the trunk of Count Olaf's car to find themselves at the Caligari Carnival. Here a den of lions messes up their day.

THE SLIPPERY SLOPE **2**

⌛ MID-1900S 🌐 THE WORLD © 2003

The Baudelaire children are split up in the Mortmain Mountains, when Sunny is kidnapped by Count Olaf. Violet and Klaus attempt to rescue her and run into an old friend and learn more about V.F.D.

THE GRIM GROTTO **2**

⌛ MID-1900S 🌐 THE WORLD © 2004

The Baudelaire children escape to the sea, where they are rescued by a submarine. But a dangerous fungus shows them who their friends really are. This is one of the best books in this miserable series.

THE PENULTIMATE PERIL **2**

⌛ MID-1900S 🌐 THE WORLD © 2005

The Baudelaire children stay at the Hotel Denouement, where they encounter a harpoon gun, a man with a beard but no hair, and a woman with hair but no beard.

THE END **2**

⌛ MID-1900S 🌐 THE WORLD © 2006

The Baudelaire children are castaways on an island. We finally get answers to some of the questions that have plagued us throughout the series.

Speare, Elizabeth George

CALICO CAPTIVE 2

⏳ MID-1700S 🌐 NEW HAMPSHIRE & CANADA © 1957

In 1754, a New Hampshire family is captured by Indians and taken to Montreal. Miriam Willard discovers what is truly important as she adjusts to her captive life. *Calico Captive* is based on a diary published in 1807.

THE WITCH OF BLACKBIRD POND 2

⏳ 1700S 🌐 CONNECTICUT © 1958

Kit's father has died, and she must move from the West Indies to live with her relatives in the Connecticut colony. She hates the strict Puritan laws of her new village. She becomes friends with an old Quaker woman who lives alone in the woods. When the village experiences a drought, they blame the old Quaker woman and hunt her down as a witch. When Kit tries to save the old woman, she is accused of witchcraft also.

THE BRONZE BOW 2

⏳ AD 30S 🌐 JUDEA © 1961

Daniel Bar Jamin is consumed with hatred for Rome and the Roman soldiers who occupy his beloved Israel. Daniel becomes involved in an outlaw band that plans insurrection. Because of his hatred and zealous patriotism, Daniel gives up everything and puts his family in great danger. When he learns of a rabbi who preaches a strange new doctrine, Daniel must choose between anger and forgiveness.

THE SIGN OF THE BEAVER 1

⏳ 1700S 🌐 MAINE © 1983

A white boy and an Indian boy become friends. The white boy is waiting for his father to return from a long journey. He teaches the reluctant Indian to read. In return, the Indian teaches him skills to survive in the wilderness.

Sperry, Armstrong

CALL IT COURAGE 1

⏳ PAST 🌐 POLYNESIAN ISLANDS © 1940

Mafatu is afraid of the sea. His friends tease him because of his fear. One day he builds a boat and ventures out alone. He is shipwrecked on an island and must survive by himself.

Spyri, Johanna

HEIDI 1

⌛ 1800S 🌐 SWITZERLAND © 1880

Heidi is brought by her aunt Dete to live with Heidi's grandfather. The grandfather lives alone in a cottage on the mountain and is feared by the villagers below. Heidi and he get along very well, and the old grandfather begins to soften under her care. One day, Dete returns to reclaim her niece. She takes Heidi to Frankfurt to work for a rich invalid girl named Klara. Heidi hates life in the city and tries to escape.

Stephens, C. A.

STORIES FROM THE OLD SQUIRE'S FARM 2

⌛ MID-1800S 🌐 MAINE © 1910

These are stories of farm life in Maine in the 1800s.

Stevenson, Robert Louis

TREASURE ISLAND 2

⌛ 1740S 🌐 ENGLAND, ATLANTIC & TROPICAL ISLAND © 1883

WARNING: If you read this book, you may never be able to enjoy any other adventure story again. You will compare it to the perfection of this book and always find it lacking. If you read this book and find it does not captivate you, then there's no hope for you. You are a truly sorry case. If you look up the word "adventure" in the dictionary, you will read "circumstances that follow the plot of *Treasure Island*."

THE BLACK ARROW 3

⌛ 1400S 🌐 ENGLAND © 1883

Dick Shelton is a trusting boy until he discovers there is foul play in the death of his father. Dick escapes from Sir Daniel's castle, but not before falling in love with Joanna Sedley. Dick becomes involved in one of the decisive battles on the side of Richard of York during the War of the Roses, but he realizes he might be on the wrong side. This book shows the growth of Dick's character from a naive boy to an experienced knight.

A CHILD'S GARDEN OF VERSES 1

⧗ LATE 1800S 🌐 ANYWHERE © 1885

These poems celebrate the best things about childhood: play, imagination, daydreams, and wonder. Robert Louis Stevenson was one of those special grown-ups who remembered what it feels like to be a child. This little book deserves to have worn edges.

KIDNAPPED 3

⧗ 1751 🌐 SCOTLAND © 1886

David Balfour visits his uncle Ebenezer to claim his father's inheritance. His uncle promises to give it to him, but he tricks David into boarding a ship first. David is taken prisoner to be sold into slavery in the Americas. On board, David meets Alan Breck, a Highlander with a price on his head. The two fight their way to shore. In Scotland, they take refuge with Alan's relatives. With the help of one of Alan's friends, David hopes to regain his inheritance.

This is a story of difficult choices and the loyalty of friends.

THE STRANGE CASE OF DR. JEKYLL AND MR. HYDE 3

⧗ MID-1800S 🌐 LONDON © 1886

Dr. Jekyll has made a new will, leaving everything to a mysterious man named Hyde. Utterson decides to investigate this Mr. Hyde. He learns Hyde is a very violent man who possesses a strange power over Dr. Jekyll.

THE BOTTLE IMP AND OTHER STORIES 2

⧗ 1800S 🌐 HAWAII © 1891

Keawe buys a bottle from a sad gentleman who says the bottle contains an imp who will grant Keawe his every wish.

CATRIONA OR DAVID BALFOUR 3

⧗ 1751 🌐 SCOTLAND, FRANCE & HOLLAND © 1893

Catriona is the sequel to *Kidnapped* and continues David Balfour's adventures as he meets the Scottish maiden Catriona, granddaughter to the famous Rob Roy.

Stowe, Harriet Beecher

UNCLE TOM'S CABIN **3**

⧗ 1850S ⊕ KENTUCKY & MISSISSIPPI © 1852

Uncle Tom's master must sell Tom down river, away from his family. Another slave, Eliza, runs away, falsely thinking her baby will be sold down river too. Tom's new master is good, but he dies and his widow sells Tom to one of the most famous villains of all time, Simon Legree. Meanwhile, Eliza travels with her child through the "underground railroad" toward Canada. When Simon Legree orders Tom to disclose the whereabouts of an escaped slave, Tom refuses and Legree beats him to unconsciousness. At the last moment, George Shelby, the son of Tom's first master, arrives on the scene.

When Stowe came to visit Abraham Lincoln, he said, "So you're the little lady who wrote the book that started this Great War." This book is one of our favorites.

Stratton-Porter, Gene

FRECKLES **1**

⧗ 1800S ⊕ INDIANA © 1904

Freckles is an orphan from Chicago. He works in the swamp guarding timber, even though he has only one hand.

A GIRL OF THE LIMBERLOST **1**

⧗ 1800S ⊕ INDIANA © 1909

Elnora Comstock lives with her mother in the Limberlost swamp. She wants to go to school, even though she has no money and her clothes are painfully unfashionable. Her mother is bitter about the death of her husband and takes her bitterness out on her daughter.

MICHAEL O'HALLORAN **2**

⧗ EARLY 1900S ⊕ MIDWEST AMERICA © 1915

Mickey is a poor boy who manages to take care of himself. One night, he finds a crippled girl and brings her to his home. She makes his life completely different, as he must think of her well-being in what he does. This book is about how he tries to make their lives better and about the people they encounter in their journey.

LADDIE: A TRUE BLUE STORY 1

1800S · INDIANA · © 1913

The Stantons live on their farm in post-Civil War Indiana. This rich narrative contains something for every reader, from nature to romance to adventure to humor. As we share daily life with the Stanton family, we come to see them as real people and good friends.

Tarkington, Booth

PENROD 1

EARLY 1900S · MIDWEST AMERICA · © 1914

Penrod Schofield is twelve and has been volunteered by his mother for *The Pageant of the Table Round* in which he is to play the "Child Sir Lancelot du Lake." He gets himself into mountains of trouble when he, at the last minute, exchanges his gaudy costume of castoff silk stockings and flannel long-johns (made by his well-meaning mother) for the janitor's overalls. Thus commences a story of boyish adventures had by Penrod and his cohort in crime, Sam Williams.

This book is one of our family's favorites to read aloud. This is one of those books that will cause you to lose your dignity and roll about the floor wheezing in agony.

PENROD AND SAM 1

EARLY 1900S · MIDWEST AMERICA · © 1916

This tells the further adventures of Penrod Schofield with his friend, Sam Williams.

PENROD JASHBER 1

EARLY 1900S · MIDWEST AMERICA · © 1929

Penrod decides to become a detective named George B. Jashber. He enlists his friend Sam Williams and two boys across the alley, Herman and Verman.

Taylor, Sydney

ALL-OF-A-KIND FAMILY 1

⧗ EARLY 1900S ⊕ NEW YORK CITY © 1951

The story of a Jewish family with five daughters living in New York City's Lower East Side. I have memories of this book being very funny.

MORE ALL-OF-A-KIND FAMILY 1

⧗ EARLY 1900S ⊕ NEW YORK CITY © 1954

This is a sequel to *All-of-a-Kind Family.* Life is never dull for sisters Ella, Henny, Sarah, Charlotte, and Gertie.

ALL-OF-A-KIND FAMILY DOWNTOWN 1

⧗ EARLY 1900S ⊕ NEW YORK CITY © 1972

This is a sequel to *All-of-a-Kind Family.* Now there is a new baby in the house, and the sisters help their mother. We meet Guido, a Italian boy who is trying to care for his sick mother.

Terhune, Albert Payson

LAD: A DOG 1

⧗ 1920S ⊕ ATLANTIC COAST OF UNITED STATES © 1920

Lad and Lady are a pair of devoted collies who, with their Master and Mistress, go through many adventures.

FURTHER ADVENTURES OF LAD 1

⧗ 1920S ⊕ ATLANTIC COAST OF UNITED STATES © 1922

This is a sequel to *Lad: A Dog.*

Tolkien, J. R. R.

THE HOBBIT 2

⧗ ANCIENT TIME ⊕ MIDDLE-EARTH © 1937

Bilbo Baggins is a little Hobbit with fur betwixt his toes. He has always been contented with life among the Hobbits, but the meddlesome wizard Gandolf tricks Bilbo into being a professional thief for thirteen irritable dwarves. The dwarves hire Bilbo to steal back their ancestral treasure from Smaug, the dragon who lives under the mountain.

This story is one of my Dad's favorites to read aloud. This book explains how Bilbo found his ring and comes before *The Lord of the Rings*.

THE LORD OF THE RINGS 3

⌛ ANCIENT TIME 🌐 MIDDLE-EARTH © 1954

Gandolf the wizard has always suspected Bilbo's golden ring is important. Now he knows it is the One Ring, the ring the dark lord is searching for. The ring can make its wearer invisible, but it will acquire an evil power over its owner. Frodo takes the ring and leaves the quiet land of Hobbits for Mount Doom, where the ring can be destroyed. On his way, Frodo gathers a fellowship of friends who want to help him.

This book is divided into three volumes: *The Fellowship of the Ring, The Two Towers,* and *The Return of the King*. As friends, Tolkien and C. S. Lewis both created fantasy worlds where real-world lessons are learned. I have to admit my mother never liked fantasy, and she refused to read this book!

Twain, Mark (Samuel L. Clemens)

THE ADVENTURES OF TOM SAWYER 2

⌛ MID-1800S 🌐 ST. PETERSBURG, MISSOURI © 1876

Tom Sawyer is an orphan living with his aunt. Tom and his friend Huck Finn visit the cemetery one night and accidentally witness Injun Joe murdering Doc Robinson. Depressed because he can not tell anyone, Tom runs away. He brings Huck with him, and they live on an island in the river. The town thinks they have drowned, but during their funeral services the boys show up, to the delight of some. At the trial of Muff Potter for the murder of the doctor, Tom points out Injun Joe as the real murderer, but Injun Joe escapes. During the town picnic, Tom and Becky explore a cave and get lost. Before finding their way out, they see Injun Joe.

This is a timeless tale of a boy's adolescence and life on the Mississippi.

THE PRINCE AND THE PAUPER 2

⌛ 1500S 🌐 ENGLAND © 1882

Tom Canty and Edward Prince of Wales are born on the same day in London. By chance, they meet and discover they look identical. The prince exchanges clothes with the beggar boy and is promptly thrown out of the palace. Tom tries to convince the courtiers that he is not the prince. Edward goes about England with Sir Miles Hendon. Miles pities the boy, thinking he is crazy. When King Henry VIII dies, the court prepares to crown Tom as King Edward VI. They hope his lack of memory about royal matters will pass. Edward is captured by Tom's father, who is a thief, and forced to endure humiliation. Edward escapes to learn his father has died. He and Miles try to reach the coronation before it is too late.

ADVENTURES OF HUCKLEBERRY FINN 2

⌛ MID-1800S ⊕ MISSISSIPPI RIVER © 1885

This is a sequel to *Tom Sawyer.* Huck Finn is adopted by the Widow Douglas, who tortures him with civilized life. He escapes but is captured by his drunken father and kept in a cabin on the river. Huck runs away down the Mississippi with Jim, the Widow Douglas's slave. Huck and Jim meet with many odd characters on their way south. Jim is captured, and Huck is mistaken for Tom Sawyer by Tom's aunt, whom Tom was to visit. Tom shows up pretending to be Sid, Tom's own brother, and they try to help Jim to escape.

Huckleberry Finn is an uncivilized river rat juggling a confused set of values and loyalties, yet he escapes ever doing wrong.

PUDD'NHEAD WILSON 3

⌛ MID-1800S ⊕ SOUTHERN AMERICA © 1893–1894

A slave woman fears for her baby's life and exchanges her light-skinned child with her master's child. From this simple act begins a mystery that will involve many lives. This is one of Twain's most complex and meaningful stories.

Verne, Jules

JOURNEY TO THE CENTER OF THE EARTH 2

⌛ MID-1800S ⊕ EUROPE, ICELAND & CENTER OF THE EARTH © 1864

Harry Lawson and Von Hardwigg discover a secret message written by the famed explorer Arne Saknussemm before he disappeared. They hire

Hans Bjelke as a guide and descend into the shaft of an extinct Icelandic volcano.

One of my favorite books. This is science fiction at its best.

IN SEARCH OF THE CASTAWAYS 2

⌛ 1860S 🌐 ENGLAND, SOUTH AMERICA, AUSTRALIA & NEW ZEALAND © 1867

Lord Glenarvan and Lady Helena are sailing their ship the *Duncan* when their crew brings up a shark with a bottle in its stomach. The bottle contains a message that appears urgent. Lord Glenarvan and Lady Helena find Mary and Robert Grand, orphans of the man who put the message in the ocean, and together they sail around the southern hemisphere searching for the castaways.

TWENTY THOUSAND LEAGUES UNDER THE SEA 2

⌛ 1866-1867 🌐 OCEANS © 1869

Professor Pierre Aronnax, his servant Conseil, and Ned Land are searching for a strange metallic fish that has been sinking ships. Their ship is rammed by the fish, and as the only survivors, they are taken aboard by Captain Nemo. Their frustration with Captain Nemo's hate for society grows. They encounter many dangers while trying to escape, including being attacked by giant squid.

Jules Verne describes technology in this story that was not invented until many years after his death.

AROUND THE WORLD IN EIGHTY DAYS 2

⌛ 1872 🌐 LONDON & AROUND THE WORLD © 1873

Phileas Fogg is a strange man, as his new valet Jean Passepartout discovers. On his first day, Fogg announces he has made a bet with friends at the Reform Club, and he and Passepartout must circumnavigate the world in exactly eighty days. The pair rushes first to Paris and then to Bombay. Passepartout notices that Mr. Fix seems to be following Mr. Fogg and learns that Fix is a detective who is trying to obtain a warrant for Fogg's arrest. While in India, they rescue the beautiful Aouda from a barbarous Hindu rite, and in the United States they are attacked by Indians. When they return to London, Fogg is arrested. It seems too late for him to win the bet.

THE MYSTERIOUS ISLAND 2

⌛ 1865-1869 🌐 SOUTH PACIFIC © 1875

Richmond, Virginia, is besieged by the Union Army, and five men escape in a balloon. They are blown out to sea by a storm and land on an island in the South Pacific. They build a good life on the island with many of their own inventions, but puzzling things happen to them. They become convinced they are not alone on the island. They save a marooned mutineer from another island and are attacked by pirates. During the battle, the pirate ship is blown out of the water by a torpedo.

This is a story of survival and hard work, interwoven with mystery. This is a sequel to *Twenty Thousand Leagues Under the Sea.*

MICHAEL STROGOFF 2

⌛ 1800S 🌐 RUSSIA © 1876

Michael Strogoff must carry a message through enemy territory to a besieged castle. I loved this story when Mother read it long ago, especially the surprise ending.

A LONG VACATION 2

⌛ 1800S 🌐 SOUTH PACIFIC © 1888

A group of boys is marooned on a deserted island in the South Pacific.

THE CASTLE OF THE CARPATHIANS 2

⌛ 1800S 🌐 TRANSYLVANIA © 1893

The village of Werst is beginning to suspect that the local castle is occupied by the devil. A visitor in the village hears the stories and decides to investigate.

Wallace, Lew

BEN-HUR 3

⌛ AD 30S 🌐 JERUSALEM, MEDITERRANEAN SEA, ROME & ANTIOCH © 1880

Judah Ben-Hur is the son of an ancient family of Israel. When his friend Messala returns from Rome, he asks Judah to betray some of the Jewish people. Judah refuses. When an accident occurs, Judah and his sister and mother are arrested. A Roman admiral releases Judah from the galleys, and Judah begins to search for his family. Filled with anger and bitterness, Judah challenges Messala to a chariot race.

Judah finds his sister and mother in the pit of the lepers. Judah discovers forgiveness when they meet Jesus on his way to the cross.

This is one of my favorite stories. *Ben-Hur* contains accurate descriptions of life in the first century AD.

Webster, Jean

DADDY-LONG-LEGS **2**

⏳ 1800S 🌐 AMERICA © 1912

Jerusha Abbott is raised in an orphanage. The headmistress tells Jerusha that one of the trustees wants to pay her way through college. Jerusha must write to him, but he doesn't want her to know his identity.

Wells, H. G.

THE TIME MACHINE **3**

⏳ LATE 1800S & AD 802,701 🌐 LONDON © 1895

The Time Traveler gathers his friends to show them a model of his time machine. He asks them to meet him a week later. Alone, he travels into the future and stops at the year AD 802,701. The world is divided into two races of people. He meets Weena, one of the simple, happy Eloi people. The Morlicks capture his time machine, but he rescues it and returns to tell his friends about his adventure. When his friends leave, he flies back into the future to save Weena from the Morlicks.

This is one of our favorites for reading aloud. Wells draws a picture of what he fears will be the evolution of humankind because of England's industrial age.

THE INVISIBLE MAN **3**

⏳ LATE 1800S 🌐 ENGLAND © 1897

A mysterious stranger asks for a room at an inn in the village of Iping. The stranger is always seen clothed in a long coat, gloves, dark spectacles, large hat, and bandages around his face. He becomes a curiosity in the village. Everybody speculates what kind of horrific deformities are under his bandages. One day, the stranger removes them, revealing "nothing, no visible thing at all."

THE WAR OF THE WORLDS 3

⏳ EARLY 1900S 🌐 ENGLAND © 1898

Early twentieth-century Martians invade Earth with giant walking machines and heat rays. The narrator describes his fight for survival and his search for his wife. When all hope seems lost, the monsters are destroyed by something very small.

White, Dale

HOLD BACK THE HUNTER 1

⏳ WEST 🌐 WESTERN AMERICA © 1959

This is a story set in Yellowstone National Park.

White, E. B.

STUART LITTLE 1

⏳ MID-1900S 🌐 NEW YORK © 1945

The Little family is surprised when their second son, Stuart, turns out to be a mouse. They thoughtfully provide ways for Stuart to function in a human world. Stuart is happy, except for his difficulties with Snowbell, the family cat. He becomes friends with a bird named Margalo; when she disappears, Stuart sets off to find her.

CHARLOTTE'S WEB 1

⏳ MID-1900S 🌐 UNITED STATES © 1952

A little girl named Fern saves a runt pig and names him Wilbur. Charlotte, the friendly spider, saves Wilbur from becoming ham by showing Fern that her pig could win a prize at the county fair. This is a classic, humorous story for children.

THE TRUMPET OF THE SWAN 1

⏳ 1900S 🌐 UNITED STATES & CANADA © 1970

Louis is a trumpeter swan of Canada who is born without a voice. He learns to read and write, but how can he tell Serena, a beautiful female swan, that he loves her? Louis's mission is to learn to play the trumpet and win Serena.

Wiggin, Kate Douglas

REBECCA OF SUNNYBROOK FARM 1

⌛ 1800S 🌐 MAINE © 1903

Leaving her family at Sunnybrook Farm, Rebecca moves in with her two spinster aunts to receive a good education.

MOTHER CAREY'S CHICKENS 2

⌛ LATE 1800S 🌐 AMERICA © 1910

Mother Carey refers to her children as her chickens. This is a story about her family.

Wilder, Laura Ingalls

LITTLE HOUSE SERIES

Laura Ingalls Wilder wanted modern children to understand what her life was like. She carefully describes the way pioneers traveled, farmed, prepared food, learned, and made friends. Laura's love for her family and admiration for her parents shines in all of her books. These are my mother's favorite stories to read aloud.

LITTLE HOUSE IN THE BIG WOODS 1

⌛ 1871 🌐 WISCONSIN © 1932

"Once upon a time, sixty years ago, a little girl lived in the Big Woods of Wisconsin, in a little gray house made of logs."

Laura tells her earliest memories of growing up in the woods of Wisconsin with Pa, Ma, and her sisters Mary and baby Carrie. She tells stories of her grandfather and a panther, hog butchering, getting a doll for Christmas, and helping her mother with household chores.

LITTLE HOUSE ON THE PRAIRIE 1

⌛ 1870S 🌐 KANSAS © 1935

The Ingalls family moves from Wisconsin to Kansas in a covered wagon. Life in a log cabin on the prairie is different from the Big Woods. They face Indians, sickness, wolves, and fire while building their new home. But they share happy times with their neighbor Mr. Edwards, explore the river nearby, and listen to Pa's fiddle under the enormous sky.

FARMER BOY 1

⌛ 1870s 🌐 NEW YORK STATE © 1933

Laura tells the story of her husband Almanzo's childhood in upstate New York. *Farmer Boy* describes a host of historic farm skills, including cutting ice, making shoes, managing oxen, and weaving. Almanzo gets into some hilarious situations.

For obvious reasons this was my favorite book of the series.

ON THE BANKS OF PLUM CREEK 1

⌛ 1870s 🌐 MINNESOTA © 1937

Laura and her family move from Kansas to Minnesota. They enjoy playing beside Plum Creek. They live near a town now, and Laura and her sister Mary are able to attend school, where Laura has a hard time with one of her classmates, the spoiled Nellie Oleson.

BY THE SHORES OF SILVER LAKE 1

⌛ 1870s 🌐 SOUTH DAKOTA © 1939

Ma, Laura, and her sisters take a train to meet Pa in Dakota Territory. They experience life in a railroad camp before spending the winter at the site of the new town of De Smet. Mary is blind from an illness, and Laura must be grown-up and responsible. Yet she relishes new adventures and experiences as her family establishes itself in their new home.

THE LONG WINTER 1

⌛ WINTER 1880 🌐 SOUTH DAKOTA © 1940

Snow covers the upstairs windows, and the Ingalls family is forced to move into town to survive. They must grind wheat for bread in a coffee grinder and twist straw for fuel. Laura and her family face their toughest battle to survive.

This was my mother's favorite of the series.

LITTLE TOWN ON THE PRAIRIE 1

⌛ 1880s 🌐 SOUTH DAKOTA © 1941

Times are better for the Ingalls family as the town of De Smet grows. Laura is busy with work, new friends, and school. She gets in trouble with her teacher Eliza Jane and catches the eye of Almanzo Wilder. The family learns about a college for the blind, and they work to send Mary there.

THESE HAPPY GOLDEN YEARS 1

⌛ 1880S 🌐 SOUTH DAKOTA © 1943

All of Laura's determination is required to get through teaching her first term of school. Almanzo Wilder picks her up every Friday so she can spend the weekend with her family. These sleigh rides begin Almanzo and Laura's courtship.

THE FIRST FOUR YEARS 2

⌛ LATE 1800S 🌐 SOUTH DAKOTA © 1971

Laura and Almanzo live on their own farm now. Together they face many obstacles in their first four years of marriage. The manuscript for this book was found after Laura Ingalls Wilder's death.

Wilson, Hazel Hutchins

THE LITTLE MARQUISE: MADAME LAFAYETTE 1

⌛ LATE 1700S 🌐 FRANCE © 1957

This is a biography of Marquis de Lafayette's wife.

Wister, Owen

THE VIRGINIAN: A HORSEMAN OF THE PLAINS 3

⌛ 1800S 🌐 WYOMING © 1902

"The Virginian's pistol came out, and his hand lay on the table, holding it unaimed. And with a voice as gentle as ever, the voice that sounded almost like a caress, but drawling a very little more than usual, so that there was almost a space between each word, he issued his orders to the man Trampas: 'When you call me that, *smile*.' And he looked at Trampas across the table."

Wodehouse, P. G.

CARRY ON, JEEVES 2

⌛ EARLY 1900S 🌐 ENGLAND © 1925

This is a collection of stories about the spineless aristocrat Bertie Wooster and his brainy valet, Jeeves. P. G. Wodehouse is one of the only authors who can use more words to say less and get away with it. His stories are so absurd and funny we can't stop reading them.

VERY GOOD, JEEVES — 2

⌛ EARLY 1900S 🌐 ENGLAND © 1930

Contains "Jeeves and the Impending Doom," "The Inferiority Complex of Old Sippy," "Jeeves and the Yule-tide Spirit," "Jeeves and the Song of Songs," "Episode of the Dog McIntosh," "The Spot of Art," "Jeeves and the Kid Clementina," "The Love That Purifies," "Jeeves and the Old School Chum," "The Indian Summer of an Uncle," and "The Ordeal of Young Tuppy."

Worline, Bonnie Bess

THE CHILDREN WHO STAYED ALONE — 1

⌛ LATE 1800S 🌐 MIDWEST AMERICA © 1965

Five children are alone in a sod house on the prairie during a blizzard.

Wren, P. C.

BEAU GESTE — 3

⌛ LATE 1800S 🌐 ENGLAND & SAHARA © 1924

A strange thing is found in the desert. Zinderneuf, a Sahara outpost, was attacked by Arabs, but when the rescuing party arrives, they find a fort full of dead men propped up in positions to look as if the fort is still defended. Thus begins a tale of bravery, a stolen jewel, and the loyalty of three brothers in the French Foreign Legion.

I know of few books that are better suited to read aloud than this book. In the end, I think my mother was crying.

BEAU SABREUR — 3

⌛ LATE 1800S 🌐 ENGLAND & SAHARA © 1926

This sequel to *Beau Geste* explains more of what happened before and after the soldiers came to Zinderneuf.

Wyss, Johann David

THE SWISS FAMILY ROBINSON — 2

⌛ LATE 1700S 🌐 EAST INDIES © 1812

After a great storm, a Swiss family find themselves the only survivors of a shipwreck. Marooned on an island, they carve out a new life using things salvaged from the ship and the tropical plants and animals. Adventure is not lacking. They build a giant tree house, endure the rainy season, tame the wild animals, are attacked by a swamp serpent, and search for other castaways. They ask themselves, "If a ship finds us, will we want to leave our island?"

This book is one of my mother's favorites. Wyss teaches children the value of hard work, natural resources, and self-reliance.

Books by Subject

Animals

Miss Hickory
–Bailey
Shasta of the Wolves
–Baker
The Adventures of Jerry Muskrat
–Burgess
The House of 60 Fathers
–De Jong
Incident at Hawk's Hill
–Eckert
Ironhead
–Ellis
The Wind in the Willows
–Grahame
All Creatures Great and Small
–Herriot
The Jungle Book
–Kipling
Ben and Me
–Lawson
Rabbit Hill
–Lawson
Gentle Ben
–Morey
Gay-Neck
–Mukerji
Rascal
–North
Animal Farm
–Orwell
The Tale of Peter Rabbit
–Potter
The Yearling
–Rawlings
Bambi
–Salten
The Rescuers
–Sharp
Charlotte's Web
–White
Stuart Little
–White
The Trumpet of the Swan
–White

Dogs

The Incredible Journey
–Burnford
A Dog of Flanders
–De La Ramee
Ginger Pye
–Estes
Old Yeller
–Gipson
Adam of the Road
–Gray
Big Red
–Kjelgaard
Irish Red
–Kjelgaard
Outlaw Red
–Kjelgaard
Lassie Come-Home
–Knight
The Call of the Wild
–London
White Fang
–London
Kavik, the Wolf Dog
–Morey
Bob, Son of Battle
–Ollivant
Daughter of the Mountains
–Rankin
Where the Red Fern Grows
–Rawls
The Hundred and One Dalmatians
–Smith
Further Adventures of Lad
–Terhune
Lad: A Dog
–Terhune

Horses

National Velvet
–Bagnold
The Black Stallion
–Farley
Born to Trot
–Henry
Justin Morgan Had a Horse
–Henry
King of the Wind
–Henry
Misty of Chincoteague
–Henry
Sea Star
–Henry
Stormy
–Henry
Smoky the Cowhorse
–James
The Horse and His Boy
–Lewis
My Friend Flicka
–O'Hara
The Blind Colt
–Rounds
Blind Outlaw
–Rounds
Whitey and the Colt Killer
–Rounds
Black Beauty
–Sewell

Wild West, Backwoods & the Rough Life

Shasta of the Wolves
–Baker
Wait for Me, Watch for Me, Eula Bee
–Beatty
Madeleine Takes Command
–Brill

The Incredible Journey
–Burnford
The Far-Off Land
–Caudill
Tree of Freedom
–Caudill
Five Bushel Farm
–Coatsworth
The Deerslayer
–Cooper
The Last of the Mohicans
–Cooper
The Courage of Sarah Noble
–Dalgliesh
Robinson Crusoe
–Defoe
The House of 60 Fathers
–De Jong
Incident at Hawk's Hill
–Eckert
The Matchlock Gun
–Edmonds
Calico Bush
–Field
Prairie Winter
–Field
The Colonials
–French
Old Yeller
–Gipson
King Solomon's Mines
–Haggard
Kon-Tiki
–Heyerdahl
Smoky the Cowhorse
–James
Komantcia
–Keith
Big Red
–Kjelgaard
Collected Short Stories of Louis L'Amour
–L'Amour
The Call of the Wild
–London
White Fang
–London
Sarah, Plain and Tall
–MacLachlan
Little Britches
–Moody
Rascal
–North
The King's Fifth
–O'Dell
Island of the Blue Dolphins
–O'Dell
The Open Range Men
–Paine
Swallows and Amazons
–Ransome
The Long Walk
–Rawicz
The Yearling
–Rawlings
The Blind Colt
–Rounds
Blind Outlaw
–Rounds
Calico Captive
–Speare
The Sign of the Beaver
–Speare
Call it Courage
–Sperry
The Mysterious Island
–Verne
Hold Back the Hunter
–White
Little House Series
–Wilder
The Children Who Stayed Alone
–Worline
The Swiss Family Robinson
–Wyss

Fairy Tales, Fantasy & Fable

Aesop's Fables
–Aesop
Andersen's Fairy Tales
–Andersen
Miss Hickory
–Bailey
Peter Pan
–Barrie
A Bear Called Paddington
–Bond
The Pilgrim's Progress
–Bunyan
Alice's Adventures in Wonderland
–Carroll
Through the Looking-Glass
–Carroll
Pinocchio
–Collodi
A Christmas Carol
–Dickens
The Reluctant Dragon
–Grahame
The Wind in the Willows
–Grahame
Grimm's Fairy Tales
–Grimm
Uncle Remus: His Songs & His Sayings
–Harris
A Wonder Book
–Hawthorne
Tanglewood Tales
–Hawthorne
Hinds' Feet on High Places
–Hurnard
The Alhambra
–Irving
The Legend of Sleepy Hollow
–Irving
Rip Van Winkle
–Irving
The Jungle Book
–Kipling
Just So Stories
–Kipling
The Boy's King Arthur
–Lanier
Ben and Me
–Lawson
Rabbit Hill
–Lawson
The Chronicles of Narnia
–Lewis
The Screwtape Letters
–Lewis
The Voyages of Doctor Dolittle
–Lofting
At the Back of the North Wind
–MacDonald
Winnie-the-Pooh
–Milne
The Little Lame Prince
–Mulock
Five Children and It
–Nesbit
The Borrowers
–Norton
Animal Farm
–Orwell
The Tale of Peter Rabbit
–Potter

The Story of King Arthur & His Knights
–Pyle
The Wonder Clock
–Pyle
The Rescuers
–Sharp
The Hundred and One Dalmatians
–Smith
A Series of Unfortunate Events
–Snicket
The Hobbit
–Tolkien
The Lord of the Rings
–Tolkien
Charlotte's Web
–White
Stuart Little
–White
The Trumpet of the Swan
–White

Family Relationships & Family Adventures

Little Men
–Alcott
Little Women
–Alcott
Emma
–Austen
Mansfield Park
–Austen
Northanger Abbey
–Austen
Persuasion
–Austen
Pride and Prejudice
–Austen
Sense and Sensibility
–Austen
Caddie Woodlawn
–Brink
Little Lord Fauntleroy
–Burnett
The Family under the Bridge
–Carlson
Dear Mr. Henshaw
–Cleary
Emily's Runaway Imagination
–Cleary
Soft Rain
–Cornelissen
The Courage of Sarah Noble
–Dalgliesh
Life With Father
–Day
Thee, Hannah!
–de Angeli
Hans Brinker
–Dodge
Incident at Hawk's Hill
–Eckert
The Matchlock Gun
–Edmonds
Ironhead
–Ellis
Ginger Pye
–Estes
Calico Bush
–Field
The Cabin Faced West
–Fritz
North and South
–Gaskell
Wives and Daughters
–Gaskell
Old Yeller
–Gipson
The Vicar of Wakefield
–Goldsmith
Born to Trot
–Henry
Stories
–Henry
Across Five Aprils
–Hunt
Mary Ellen
–Justus
The Trumpeter of Krakow
–Kelly
The Victory Garden
–Kochenderfer
To Kill a Mockingbird
–Lee
Shoo-Fly Girl
–Lenski
Strawberry Girl
–Lenski
Number the Stars
–Lowry
Sarah, Plain and Tall
–MacLachlan
Anne of Avonlea
–Montgomery
Anne of Green Gables
–Montgomery
Mistress Pat
–Montgomery
Pat of Silver Bush
–Montgomery
Little Britches
–Moody
The Railway Children
–Nesbit
The Story of the Treasure Seekers
–Nesbit
Pollyanna
–Porter
Swallows & Amazons
–Ransome
The Yearling
–Rawlings
Three Go Searching
–St. John
Treasures of the Snow
–St. John
The Good Master
–Seredy
The Little Riders
–Shemin
Calico Captive
–Speare
Heidi
–Spyri
Laddie: A True Blue Story
–Stratton-Porter
Penrod
–Tarkington
Penrod Jashber
–Tarkington
Penrod & Sam
–Tarkington
All-of-a-Kind Family
–Taylor
Little House Series
–Wilder
Swiss Family Robinson
–Wyss

Friendship

Emma
–Austen
Mansfield Park
–Austen
Northanger Abbey
–Austen
Pride and Prejudice
–Austen
The Secret Garden
–Burnett

The Family under the Bridge
–Carlson
Dear Mr. Henshaw
–Cleary
Ellen Tebbits
–Cleary
The House of 60 Fathers
–De Jong
I, Juan de Pareja
–de Treviño
The Hundred Dresses
–Estes
The Cabin Faced West
–Fritz
Wives and Daughters
–Gaskell
The Wind in the Willows
–Grahame
Good-bye Mr. Chips
–Hilton
Across Five Aprils
–Hunt
Mary Ellen
–Justus
To Kill a Mockingbird
–Lee
The Chronicles of Narnia
–Lewis
Number the Stars
–Lowry
Winnie-the-Pooh
–Milne
Anne of Avonlea
–Montgomery
Anne of Green Gables
–Montgomery
Mistress Pat
–Montgomery
Pat of Silver Bush
–Montgomery
Pollyanna
–Porter
Three Go Searching
–St. John
Treasures of the Snow
–St. John
The Rescuers
–Sharp
Laddie: A True Blue Story
–Stratton-Porter
Michael O'Halloran
–Stratton-Porter
Charlotte's Web
–White
Stuart Little
–White

Humorous

The Story of a Bad Boy
–Aldrich
Miss Hickory
–Bailey
A Bear Called Paddington
–Bond
Alice's Adventures in Wonderland
–Carroll
Through the Looking-Glass
–Carroll
Ellen Tebbits
–Cleary
Emily's Runaway Imagination
–Cleary
Life With Father
–Day
The Wind in the Willows
–Grahame
Uncle Remus: His Songs & His Sayings
–Harris
Stories
–Henry
All Creatures Great and Small
–Herriot
The Legend of Sleepy Hollow
–Irving
Rip Van Winkle
–Irving
Ben and Me
–Lawson
The Screwtape Letters
–Lewis
Homer Price
–McCloskey
Now We are Six
–Milne
When We Were Very Young
–Milne
Winnie-the-Pooh
–Milne
Five Children and It
–Nesbit
The Railway Children
–Nesbit
The Story of the Treasure Seekers
–Nesbit
The Borrowers Series
–Norton
The Tale of Peter Rabbit
–Potter
The Rescuers
–Sharp
Five Little Peppers
–Sidney
The Hundred and One Dalmatians
–Smith
A Series of Unfortunate Events
–Snicket
Penrod
–Tarkington
Penrod Jashber
–Tarkington
Penrod and Sam
–Tarkington
All-of-a-Kind Family
–Taylor
The Adventures of Tom Sawyer
–Twain
Stuart Little
–White
The Trumpet of the Swan
–White
Carry on, Jeeves
–Wodehouse
Very Good, Jeeves
–Wodehouse

Young Heroine

The Wolves of Willoughby Chase
–Aiken
National Velvet
–Bagnold
Toliver's Secret
–Brady
Madeleine Takes Command
–Brill
Caddie Woodlawn
–Brink
A Little Princess
–Burnett
The Secret Garden
–Burnett
Alice's Adventures in Wonderland
–Carroll
Through the Looking-Glass
–Carroll
Tree of Freedom
–Caudill

Ellen Tebbits
–Cleary
Emily's Runaway Imagination
–Cleary
Ramona Quimby, Age 8
–Cleary
Soft Rain
–Cornelissen
The Terrible Wave
–Dahlstedt
The Courage of Sarah Noble
–Dalgliesh
Thee, Hannah!
–de Angeli
The Hundred Dresses
–Estes
Calico Bush
–Field
Hepatica Hawks
–Field
Hitty: Her First Hundred Years
–Field
Understood Betsy
–Fisher
The Cabin Faced West
–Fritz
Goody Two-Shoes
–Goldsmith
Katrinka
–Haskell
Misty of Chincoteague
–Henry
Lucinda, a Little Girl of 1860
–Hunt
Mary Ellen
–Justus
The Victory Garden
–Kochenderfer
To Kill a Mockingbird
–Lee
Shoo-Fly Girl
–Lenski
Strawberry Girl
–Lenski
The Chronicles of Narnia
–Lewis
Number the Stars
–Lowry
The Adventures of Perrine
–Malot
Anne of Avonlea
–Montgomery
Anne of Green Gables
–Montgomery
Mistress Pat
–Montgomery
Pat of Silver Bush
–Montgomery
The Lost Queen of Egypt
–Morrison
The Railway Children
–Nesbit
The Borrowers Series
–Norton
Island of the Blue Dolphins
–O'Dell
Pollyanna
–Porter
Pollyanna Grows Up
–Porter
Cinder Pond
–Rankin
Daughter of the Mountains
–Rankin
Gypsy Nan
–Rankin
Swallows and Amazons
–Ransome
Elli of the Northland
–Ruthin
Treasures of the Snow
–St. John
The Good Master
–Seredy
The Little Riders
–Shemin
Calico Captive
–Speare
The Witch of Blackbird Pond
–Speare
Heidi
–Spyri
A Girl of the Limberlost
–Stratton-Porter
Daddy-Long-Legs
–Webster
Charlotte's Web
–White
Rebecca of Sunnybrook Farm
–Wiggin
Little House Series
–Wilder

Young Hero

The Story of a Bad Boy
–Aldrich
Tom the Bootblack
–Alger
Shasta of the Wolves
–Baker
Master Skylark
–Bennett
Lorna Doone
–Blackmore
Little Lord Fauntleroy
–Burnett
The Lost Prince
–Burnett
Dear Mr. Henshaw
–Cleary
Pinocchio
–Collodi
Black Fox of Lorne
–de Angeli
The Door in the Wall
–de Angeli
The House of 60 Fathers
–De Jong
A Dog of Flanders
–de la Ramée
Oliver Twist
–Dickens
Hans Brinker
–Dodge
Incident At Hawk's Hill
–Eckert
The Matchlock Gun
–Edmonds
Ironhead
–Ellis
The Black Stallion
–Farley
Johnny Tremain
–Forbes
Old Yeller
–Gipson
Adam of the Road
–Gray
Justin Morgan Had a Horse
–Henry
King of the Wind
–Henry
Misty of Chincoteague
–Henry
By Right of Conquest
–Henty
North to Freedom
–Holm
Tom Brown's School Days
–Hughes
Across Five Aprils
–Hunt

The Trumpeter of Krakow
–Kelly

Captains Courageous
–Kipling

The Jungle Book
–Kipling

Kim
–Kipling

Big Red
–Kjelgaard

Irish Red
–Kjelgaard

Lassie Come-Home
–Knight

Carry On, Mr. Bowditch
–Latham

The Buccaneers
–Lawrence

The Smugglers
–Lawrence

The Wreckers
–Lawrence

The Chronicles of Narnia
–Lewis

Young Fu of the Upper Yangtze
–Lewis

Tales of the Fish Patrol
–London

At the Back of the North Wind
–MacDonald

Sir Gibbie
–MacDonald

The Adventures of Remi
–Malot

Homer Price
–McCloskey

Little Britches
–Moody

Gentle Ben
–Morey

Kavik, the Wolf Dog
–Morey

The Little Lame Prince
–Mulock

The Railway Children
–Nesbit

Rascal
–North

The Black Pearl
–O'Dell

My Friend Flicka
–O'Hara

Toby Tyler
–Otis

Long Wharf
–Pease

Men of Iron
–Pyle

Otto of the Silver Hand
–Pyle

Swallows and Amazons
–Ransome

The Yearling
–Rawlings

Where the Red Fern Grows
–Rawls

The Blind Colt
–Rounds

Holes
–Sachar

Three Go Searching
–St. John

Twice Freed
–St. John

The Good Master
–Seredy

Theras and His Town
–Snedeker

The Sign of the Beaver
–Speare

Call It Courage
–Sperry

Kidnapped
–Stevenson

Treasure Island
–Stevenson

Michael O'Halloran
–Stratton-Porter

Penrod
–Tarkington

Lad: A Dog
–Terhune

Adventures of Huckleberry Finn
–Twain

The Adventures of Tom Sawyer
–Twain

The Prince and the Pauper
–Twain

In Search of the Castaways
–Verne

Farmer Boy
–Wilder

The Little Marquise
–Wilson

Swiss Family Robinson
–Wyss

Maturing Character

Jane Eyre
–Brontë

The Last Days of Pompeii
–Bulwer-Lytton

The Pilgrim's Progress
–Bunyan

The Secret Garden
–Burnett

Dear Mr. Henshaw
–Cleary

Pinocchio
–Collodi

The Terrible Wave
–Dahlstedt

The Door in the Wall
–de Angeli

Thee, Hannah!
–de Angeli

Black Fox of Lorne
–de Angeli

Robinson Crusoe
–Defoe

Incident at Hawk's Hill
–Eckert

Silas Marner
–Eliot

The Hundred Dresses
–Estes

Understood Betsy
–Fisher

Johnny Tremain
–Forbes

The Story of Rolf and the Viking Bow
–French

North and South
–Gaskell

Wives and Daughters
–Gaskell

Stories
–Henry

Tom Brown's School Days
–Hughes

Les Misérables
–Hugo

Across Five Aprils
–Hunt

Captains Courageous
–Kipling

The Horse and His Boy
–Lewis

The Silver Chair
–Lewis

The Voyage of the Dawn Treader
–Lewis
Anne of Avonlea
–Montgomery
Anne of Green Gables
–Montgomery
Mistress Pat
–Montgomery
Pat of Silver Bush
–Montgomery
The Little Lame Prince
–Mulock
Stepping Heavenward
–Prentiss
The Yearling
–Rawlings
Treasures of the Snow
–St. John
Twice Freed
–St. John
The Bronze Bow
–Speare
Calico Captive
–Speare
Call it Courage
–Sperry
The Black Arrow
–Stevenson
Laddie: A True Blue Story
–Stratton-Porter
Ben-Hur
–Wallace

Mystery

The Wolves of Willoughby Chase
–Aiken
The Thirty-Nine Steps
–Buchan
The Moonstone
–Collins
The Woman in White
–Collins
Our Mutual Friend
–Dickens
The Adventures of Sherlock Holmes
–Doyle
The Case-Book of Sherlock Holmes
–Doyle
His Last Bow
–Doyle
The Hound of the Baskervilles
–Doyle
The Memoirs of Sherlock Holmes
–Doyle
The Return of Sherlock Holmes
–Doyle
The Sign of the Four
–Doyle
A Study in Scarlet
–Doyle
The Valley of Fear
–Doyle
The House of the Seven Gables
–Hawthorne
The Scarlet Pimpernel
–Orczy
Red Rock
–Page
Holes
–Sachar
Three Go Searching
–St. John
A Series of Unfortunate Events
–Snicket
The Strange Case of Dr. Jekyll and Mr. Hyde
–Stevenson
Pudd'nhead Wilson
–Twain
The Mysterious Island
–Verne
Beau Geste
–Wren
Beau Sabreur
–Wren

Middle East & Asia

The House of 60 Fathers
–De Jong
The Alhambra
–Irving
Kim
–Kipling
Anna and the King of Siam
–Landon
When the Typhoon Blows
–Lewis
Young Fu of the Upper Yangtze
–Lewis
The Lost Queen of Egypt
–Morrison
Gay-Neck
–Mukerji
Daughter of the Mountains
–Rankin
The Long Walk
–Rawicz
The Talisman
–Scott
The White Stag
–Serdey
The Bronze Bow
–Speare
Around the World in Eighty Days
–Verne
Michael Strogoff
–Verne
Ben-Hur
–Wallace
Beau Geste
–Wren
Beau Sabreur
–Wren

Pioneers

Wait for Me, Watch for Me, Eula Bee
–Beatty
Caddie Woodlawn
–Brink
Magical Melons
–Brink
The Far-Off Land
–Caudill
Tree of Freedom
–Caudill
Five Bushel Farm
–Coatsworth
The Deerslayer
–Cooper
The Last of the Mohicans
–Cooper
The Courage of Sarah Noble
–Dalgliesh
Incident at Hawk's Hill
–Eckert
The Matchlock Gun
–Edmonds
Winter Journey
–Falk
Calico Bush
–Field

Prairie Winter
–Field
The Cabin Faced West
–Fritz
Old Yeller
–Gipson
Head to the West
–Hoff
Collected Short Stories of Louis L'Amour
–L'Amour
The Call of the Wild
–London
Sarah, Plain and Tall
–MacLachlan
Little Britches
–Moody
Captured by the Mohawks
–North
The Open Range Men
–Paine
The Oregon Trail
–Parkman
The Yearling
–Rawlings
Calico Captive
–Speare
The Sign of the Beaver
–Speare
Little House Series
–Wilder
The Virginian
–Wister
The Children Who Stayed Alone
–Worline
The Swiss Family Robinson
–Wyss

Science Fiction

The Lost World
–Doyle
The Twenty-One Balloons
–Du Bois
Chitty Chitty Bang Bang
–Fleming
The Strange Case of Dr. Jekyll and Mr. Hyde
–Stevenson
Journey to the Center of the Earth
–Verne
The Mysterious Island
–Verne
Twenty Thousand Leagues Under the Sea
–Verne
The Invisible Man
–Wells
The Time Machine
–Wells
The War of the Worlds
–Wells

Sea

Robinson Crusoe
–Defoe
The Man Without a Country
–Hale
The Dark Frigate
–Hawes
The Mutineers
–Hawes
Wreck Ashore
–Heatter
Kon-Tiki
–Heyerdahl
Captains Courageous
–Kipling
Carry on, Mr. Bowditch
–Latham
The Buccaneers
–Lawrence
The Smugglers
–Lawrence
The Wreckers
–Lawrence
The Voyage of the Dawn Treader
–Lewis
Moby-Dick
–Melville
The Black Pearl
–O'Dell
Island of the Blue Dolphins
–O'Dell
Long Wharf
–Pease
Shipwreck
–Pease
Within the Capes
–Pyle
Swallows and Amazons
–Ransome
John Holdsworth; Chief Mate
–Russell
The Wreck of the Grosvenor
–Russell
The Grim Grotto
–Snicket
Call it Courage
–Sperry
Treasure Island
–Stevenson
In Search of the Castaways
–Verne
A Long Vacation
–Verne
The Mysterious Island
–Verne
Twenty Thousand Leagues Under the Sea
–Verne
The Swiss Family Robinson
–Wyss

Ancient

Martyr of the Catacombs
–Anonymous
Shasta of the Wolves
–Baker
The Last Days of Pompeii
–Bulwer-Lytton
Cat of the Bubastes
– Henty
The Lost Queen of Egypt
–Morrison
Twice Freed
–St. John
The White Stag
–Seredy
Luke's Quest
–Snedeker
Theras and His Town
–Snedeker
The Bronze Bow
–Speare
Ben-Hur
–Wallace

Medieval

Twice Queen of France
–Butler
Black Fox of Lorne
–de Angeli
The Door in the Wall
–de Angeli

The White Company
–Doyle
The Red Keep
–French
Lost Baron
–French
The Story of Rolf and the Viking Bow
–French
Adam of the Road
–Gray
St. George for England
–Henty
The Trumpeter of Krakow
–Kelly
The Boy's King Arthur
–Lanier
Journey for a Princess
–Leighton
Judith of France
–Leighton
The Scottish Chiefs
–Porter
Men of Iron
–Pyle
The Merry Adventures of Robin Hood
–Pyle
Otto of the Silver Hand
–Pyle
The Story of King Arthur and his Knights
–Pyle
Ivanhoe
–Scott
Quentin Durward
–Scott
The Talisman
–Scott
The Black Arrow
–Stevenson

Renaissance & Reformation

Master Skylark
–Bennett
Lorna Doone
–Blackmore
I, Juan de Pareja
–de Treviño
Tales From Shakespeare
–Lamb
The Hawk That Dare Not Hunt by Day
–O'Dell
The King's Fifth
–O'Dell
The Prince and the Pauper
–Twain

American Revolution

Drums
–Boyd
Toliver's Secret
–Brady
Johnny Tremain
–Forbes
The Colonials
–French
Treasure of the Revolution
–Fox
Ben and Me
–Lawson

French Revolution

A Tale of Two Cities
–Dickens
Eldorado
–Orczy
The Elusive Pimpernel
–Orczy
The League of the Scarlet Pimpernel
–Orczy
The Scarlet Pimpernel
–Orczy
The Little Marquise
–Wilson

Civil War

Little Women
–Alcott
I Want My Sunday, Stranger!
–Beatty
Cadmus Henry
–Edmonds
Across Five Aprils
–Hunt
Lucinda, a Little Girl of 1860
–Hunt
Rifles for Watie
–Keith
In Ole Virginia
–Page
Red Rock
–Page
Two Confederates
–Page
Uncle Tom's Cabin
–Stowe

World War One

Adventures of Richard Hannay
–Buchan
Thirty-Nine Steps
–Buchan
Gay-Neck
–Mukerji

World War Two

Twenty and Ten
–Bishop
The House of 60 Fathers
–De Jong
All Creatures Great and Small
–Herriot
North to Freedom
–Holm
The Victory Garden
–Kochenderfer
Number the Stars
–Lowry
The Long Walk
–Rawicz
The Silver Sword
–Serraillier
The Little Riders
–Shemin